Winning at the Table

A COLLECTION OF FAVORITE RECIPES
FROM THE JUNIOR LEAGUE OF LAS VEGAS

All proceeds from *Winning at the Table* will be returned to the community through projects supported by the Junior League of Las Vegas.

Additional copies may be obtained from the Junior League of Las Vegas, Inc. by mailing the order form at the back of the book.

First Printing • May, 1985 • 20,000 copies

Second Printing • December, 1987 • 10,000 copies

ISBN 0-9614100-1-9

Printed by Hart Graphics
Austin, Texas

The Cookbook Committee

Chairman	Priscilla Scalley
Editor	Marti Hafen
Recipe Collection and Testing	Christy Jones, Chairman
	Linda Casey
	Lynne Freeman
	Mary Jo Miller
Format	Lynn Wirth, Chairman
	Luanne Glenn
	Gretchen Winchester
Marketing	Nancy Joslin, Chairman
	Pam Brown
	Pamela Wald

The Junior League of Las Vegas gratefully acknowledges . . .

Larry Hanna Photography	Photography
Patty Coluse	Cover Design and Graphics

. . . for their expertise in the development of this cookbook.

We dedicate this book to those who have made and those who continue to make our city a warm and hospitable place in which to live.

Las Vegas

The initial impression of present-day Las Vegas is in vivid contrast to the scene which welcomed the travelers of the 1800s. The first recorded history dates to 1830, when it was written that the valley's rushing springs provided a water supply for nomadic Indians as well as trade caravans winding their way west along the Spanish Trail from Santa Fe to the California seaboard. The surrounding meadows provided grazing for the travelers' stock and welcome respite from the otherwise vast and barren desert. Spanish traders called this oasis "Las Vegas", meaning "the meadows". The future held great promise for a permanent settlement here because of the abundance of water. Water was the essential ingredient needed to support the development of a lasting community. However, twenty years would pass before anything more than a re-mounting station for the Pony Express would be established.

Then, in the early 1850s a diversified group of thirty Mormons were sent by the church to farm the Las Vegas Valley and convert the local Paiute Indians to the Mormon faith. The mission survived until 1857 when internal bickering and an uncertainty over leadership resulted in most of the settlers abandoning the outpost and returning to Salt Lake City. Once again the valley was only a water stop for traders and Indians.

It was not until 1882 that several pioneer families founded the settlement that would evolve into the Las Vegas we know today. The Stewart Ranch, located on the site of the present-day business district, was the nucleus of this young farming community. The Stewarts, along with neighboring ranchers, launched the area's reputation for western hospitality by opening their homes to weary travelers. These first "tourists" to the Las Vegas Valley were prospectors and miners who sought their fortune in the nearby mountains of Southern Nevada. However, farming and ranching would continue to support the area's economic base throughout the balance of the 19th century.

With the onset of the 20th century a handful of permanent residents anticipated construction of the long-awaited railroad which would change the course of Las Vegas history. In the summer of 1904 steel rails were progressing rapidly through the sagebrush-laden valley to connect Salt Lake City to Los Angeles. The terrain of the area, the prevalence of timber in the nearby mountains and—*water*—were the crucial factors in the decision to route the railroad through Las Vegas. As the rails traversed the desert, tent saloons, stores and boarding houses cropped up to cope with the expanded population of 1,500.

On the morning of May 15, 1905 the railroad placed 1200 lots comprising the Las Vegas Townsite on the auction block. Over a thousand land-hungry purchasers gathered in the wilting 106° heat to make their bids, and by evening the commotion of construction had begun on the newly purchased lots. Las Vegas was officially born.

By 1920 an era of stability had begun with 2,000 full-time residents vitally interested in promoting their town's expansion and welfare. Trees were planted, sidewalks were built, and automobiles traveled the now-oiled streets. A city of tents had blossomed into an established railroad town whose residents graciously opened their spare rooms to visitors when the hotels were full. By 1927 Las Vegas could be reached by train, car and even plane. The increasing influx of visitors began to form a fledgling tourism industry.

In 1930 the Federal Government chose a site near Las Vegas for the Hoover Dam Project. A work force of 10,000 men began construction in nearby Black Canyon to provide flood control on the Colorado River and to create a tremendous source of energy. Just as the Depression was striking its economic blow throughout the country, Las Vegas began the monumental task of building highways and homes to cope with the expanding number of residents.

1931 marked the repeal of an act which had outlawed gambling in Nevada since 1909. In the early mining days gambling had been second nature to the miners with their new-found wealth and desire for entertainment. Then the Legislature outlawed all but a few card games from 1909 to 1931. Since 1931, amendments to the gaming act have allowed for taxation, strict licensing and regulatory controls over legalized gaming establishments.

Nellis Air Force Base was established on January 25, 1941 and brought thousands of military personnel to the Las Vegas area. During the height of World War II, 600 gunnery students and 215 copilots graduated every five weeks from Nellis. Since then the base has played an important role in the training of Air Force pilots. Today it serves as the largest tactical Air Force base in the free world and is home to the Thunderbirds—the United States Air Force Precision Flying Team. Nellis is a powerful economic influence on

Southern Nevada, employing thousands of personnel, many of whom make Las Vegas their permanent home when they leave the Air Force.

Another government related influence on the growth of Las Vegas has been the Nevada Test Site, located about sixty miles north of the city. Many of the local scientific and industrial companies were established as a result of nuclear-weapons testing and related programs at the Test Site.

Legalized gaming, Nellis Air Force Base and the Nevada Test Site all affected the dramatic growth of Las Vegas in the 1940s and 1950s. With the town's burgeoning population and increased interest in tourism stimulated by Hoover Dam, the need arose for hotels catering to the traveling public. Furthermore, after World War II, people who had been pent-up by the wartime economy were ready to travel. A cursory count of traffic entering Las Vegas proved enough for one man to build the first resort hotel, El Rancho Vegas. He selected a site on the southernmost edge of town on the highway to Los Angeles, near the present intersection of Sahara Avenue and Las Vegas Boulevard. Many other entrepreneurs followed suit, and a vast array of hotels and casinos were built along this route, which eventually became the world-famous "Las Vegas Strip".

Las Vegas was soon regarded as "the entertainment and resort capital of the world". Billboards, magazines, television and radio carried the message to people everywhere that Las Vegas was a vacation paradise with an easy-going western life style, exciting night life and scenic wonders. Lavish shows and name entertainers continue to draw capacity crowds to this desert mecca.

Today Las Vegans enjoy a broad spectrum of recreational and cultural activities. The mild climate permits participation in outdoor sports on a year-round basis. Cultural activities encompass the ballet, symphony and theatre. The University of Nevada, Las Vegas offers all levels of collegiate education and has an excellent curriculum in hotel administration. Residents enjoy a wealth of Southwestern scenery. Nearby attractions include Lake Mead, Red Rock Canyon, Mount Charleston and the Valley of Fire. In addition, the Grand Canyon, Death Valley and Southern Utah's many national parks are all near enough for weekend excursions. Today Las Vegas is one of the fastest growing cities in the United States. What was once an oasis to nomadic Indians and the trade caravans of the mid-1800s is now home to approximately 500,000 residents.

Table of Contents

Appetizers
and Beverages

SHRIMP CUPS

Our filled shrimp cups can be frozen. Defrost 1 hour before broiling.

12 slices white bread, crusts removed
    melted butter or margarine
⅔ cup mayonnaise
⅓ cup freshly grated Parmesan cheese
⅓ cup shredded Swiss cheese
⅓ cup chopped green onions
¼ teaspoon Worcestershire sauce
2 drops Tabasco
¾ cup chopped cooked shrimp

Using a rolling pin, roll bread slices as flat as possible. With a 2½ or 3-inch round biscuit or cookie cutter, cut 2 rounds from each slice of bread. Lightly brush each round with melted butter. Line 24 small muffin cups with the bread rounds and bake in a preheated 350° oven until golden. In a medium-size bowl combine mayonnaise, Parmesan cheese, Swiss cheese, onions, Worcestershire, Tabasco and shrimp. Mix well. Fill bread cups with this mixture and broil about 4 to 6 minutes until hot.

Makes 24

CROQUE GUILLAUME

1 loaf French bread
2 tablespoons flour
1 egg
½ cup dry white wine
1 cup grated Swiss cheese
½ cup diced cooked ham
1 teaspoon Dijon-style mustard
½ teaspoon salt
⅛ teaspoon cayenne pepper
    freshly ground pepper
4 tablespoons butter, melted

Cut loaf of bread in half horizontally. Place cut sides up on a baking sheet and dry out in a preheated 350° oven for 20 minutes. Remove and increase oven temperature to 450°. In a mixing bowl blend flour, egg and wine. Mix in grated cheese, ham, mustard, salt, cayenne and pepper. Brush bread with melted butter, then spread with the cheese mixture. Bake in the 450° oven for 15 to 20 minutes or until lightly browned. To serve, cool slightly, cut bread in half lengthwise, and then crosswise into 1½-inch wide pieces.

Makes 16 to 18

PEPPERONI CHEESE BITES

This recipe doubles nicely and freezes well. To reheat, place cheese bites in a shallow pan and bake in a preheated 375° oven for 6 minutes or until heated through.

½ 10-ounce package frozen chopped spinach, thawed and drained
1 cup ricotta cheese
¾ cup freshly grated Parmesan cheese
⅔ cup finely chopped mushrooms
2 tablespoons finely chopped onion
½ teaspoon oregano
¼ teaspoon salt
1 egg
24 slices pepperoni
   diced pepperoni (optional)
   sour cream (optional)

Lightly grease 24 1-inch muffin cups. In a bowl combine spinach, ricotta cheese, Parmesan cheese, mushrooms, onion, oregano, salt and egg. Place one slice of pepperoni in the bottom of each muffin cup. Spoon cheese mixture into cups and bake in a preheated 375° oven for 25 minutes or until lightly golden. Cool 10 minutes and gently remove cheese bites from muffin cups. Serve warm or cold. If desired, garnish with diced pepperoni and sour cream.

Makes 24

WALNUT ROQUEFORT CANAPÉS

4 ounces Roquefort or blue cheese
4 tablespoons butter, softened
⅓ cup finely chopped walnuts
½ teaspoon salt
   pepper
1 tablespoon Cognac
36 Melba toast rounds
36 walnut halves

In a mixing bowl blend cheese with butter. Stir in chopped walnuts, salt, pepper and Cognac. Using a pastry bag with a large fluted tip, place a rosette of cheese mixture on each toast round. Press a walnut half into the center and serve.

Makes 36

CANAPÉS À LA FLORENTINE

1   10-ounce package frozen spinach, cooked and drained
1   medium onion, chopped
2   tablespoons butter or margarine
3   tablespoons flour
1   cup milk
½   teaspoon salt
¼   teaspoon white pepper
¼   teaspoon nutmeg
⅛   teaspoon cayenne pepper
32   Melba toast rounds
½   cup freshly grated Parmesan cheese

Thoroughly pat dry drained spinach. Finely chop spinach and set aside. In a heavy saucepan sauté onion in butter until soft but not brown. Add flour and cook for 2 minutes stirring constantly. In a separate saucepan scald the milk. Blend milk into flour mixture while stirring vigorously with a wire whisk. Bring to a boil and continue stirring for 1 minute. Add spinach, salt, pepper, nutmeg and cayenne. Stir and simmer for 5 minutes or until very thick. Immediately before serving, spread mixture on toast rounds and sprinkle with Parmesan cheese. Place canapés on a cookie sheet and bake in a preheated 400° oven until lightly brown.

Makes 32

CRAB MEAT SPREAD

In testing this recipe we found that it was particularly popular with men. The red and green colors of the chili sauce and parsley make a festive presentation of this appetizer at holiday time.

12   ounces cream cheese, softened
1   tablespoon Worcestershire sauce
1   tablespoon lemon juice
2   tablespoons mayonnaise
1   small onion, finely grated
  dash of garlic salt
½   pound cooked crabmeat, flaked
6   ounces chili sauce
  chopped fresh parsley

In a bowl combine cream cheese, Worcestershire sauce, lemon juice, mayonnaise, onion, garlic salt and crabmeat. Mix well. Spread in a shallow serving dish. Pour chili sauce over crab mixture. Garnish with parsley and refrigerate until ready to serve. Accompany with crackers.

Serves 15

CLAM FILLED SHEPHERDS BREAD

1 whole round loaf Shepherds bread
3 6½-ounce cans minced clams
16 ounces cream cheese, softened
2 tablespoons chopped green onions
¼ teaspoon Tabasco
2 tablespoons Worcestershire sauce
2 teaspoons lemon juice

Using a serrated knife, cut a lid off the top of the Shepherds bread. Pull out the bread from the inside, leaving a hollow loaf. Allow the inner bread pieces to dry at room temperature or toast lightly in the oven. Set aside. Drain clams, reserving the juice from 1 can. In a bowl mix together clams, the reserved clam juice, cream cheese, green onions, Tabasco, Worcestershire and lemon juice. Pour this mixture into the bread shell and replace the bread lid. Wrap with foil and place on a cookie sheet. Bake in a preheated 350° oven for 1 hour. Serve loaf on a large round tray and surround with the dried bread pieces to use as dippers. You can also break away the bread shell and use it for dipping.

Serves 10

CHUTNEY CHEESE BALLS

These cheese balls may be frozen for up to three months. Allow them to thaw 2 to 3 hours before serving.

24 ounces cream cheese, softened
1 cup sour cream
1 cup chopped raisins
1 cup chopped salted peanuts
8 slices bacon, cooked and crumbled
½ cup chopped green onion
4 teaspoons curry powder
   chutney
   shredded coconut
   finely minced parsley

Combine cream cheese, sour cream, raisins, peanuts, bacon, green onion and curry powder. Mix well. Shape into two large balls. Wrap in plastic wrap and refrigerate. Before serving, top the cheese balls with chutney. Sprinkle with shredded coconut and parsley. Serve with crackers.

Makes 2

CHEESE FILLED PASTRY PUFFS

These pastry puffs can be used with a sweet dessert filling if you omit the Parmesan cheese from the recipe. They freeze beautifully; simply thaw just before filling.

¾ cup water
6 tablespoons butter or margarine
pinch of salt
¾ cup flour
3 eggs
freshly grated Parmesan cheese

In a saucepan heat water, butter and salt to boiling. Add flour all at once and stir briskly until mixture forms a ball. Remove from heat and add eggs one at a time, beating well after each addition. Drop by teaspoons onto a greased cookie sheet. Sprinkle tops with Parmesan cheese and bake in a preheated 400° oven 25 to 30 minutes or until nicely puffed and dry. Cool.

FILLING

8 ounces cream cheese, softened
1 chicken bouillon cube, crushed
1 tablespoon minced onion
¼ cup heavy cream
1 2¼-ounce can sliced black olives

In a bowl mix cream cheese, bouillon, onion, cream and olives. Slice cooled pastry puffs in half horizontally and fill with cheese mixture.

Makes 40

When setting a distinctive-looking table, don't always stick to things that belong in the dining room. Take your favorite piece of sculpture from the living room or that large basket you purchased in the country to use as a centerpiece.

LIPTAUER CHEESE AND PUMPERNICKEL

This Liptauer cheese may be prepared and refrigerated for up to four days before serving. The recipe's contributor noted that it also makes an excellent spread for breakfast toast.

16 ounces cream cheese,
 softened
5 ounces sharp Cheddar cheese,
 room temperature
4 tablespoons butter, softened
1 teaspoon Dijon-style mustard
1½ tablespoons chopped onion
 paprika

Combine cheeses, butter, mustard and onion in a food processor. Process until smooth. Shape into a ball and sprinkle with paprika.

ACCOMPANIMENTS

chopped anchovies
finely chopped green onions
chopped cucumber
drained capers
pumpernickel bread

To serve, place garnishes in small bowls and accompany with pumpernickel bread.

Serves 12

STUFFED ARTICHOKE HEARTS

Don't hesitate to assemble this appetizer in advance. Simply cover and refrigerate until ready to bake.

5 7-ounce cans whole hearts of
 small artichokes
8 ounces cream cheese,
 softened
¼ cup finely chopped green
 onion
¼ teaspoon garlic salt
⅛ teaspoon pepper
4 tablespoons butter, melted
 freshly grated Parmesan
 cheese

Drain artichoke hearts and slice off the bottom tip so that hearts stand upright. In a bowl combine cream cheese, green onion, garlic salt and pepper. Mound mixture evenly on top of artichoke hearts. Roll hearts in melted butter and then Parmesan cheese. Place in a shallow ovenproof dish and bake in a preheated 400° oven for 15 minutes or until hot and bubbly.

Makes 30

BRANDIED MUSHROOMS

24 whole medium-size
mushrooms
1 cup butter, melted
2 small onions, chopped
3 garlic cloves, minced
½ cup minced parsley
2 tablespoons flour
½ cup seasoned bread crumbs
1 cup sour cream
salt
pepper
brandy
freshly grated Parmesan
cheese
Sauterne wine

Remove and chop mushroom stems. In a medium-size bowl combine chopped stems, butter, onions, garlic and parsley. Mix well. Add flour, bread crumbs, sour cream, salt and pepper. Blend well. Arrange mushroom caps hollow side up in a shallow baking dish. Drizzle a small amount of brandy in each cap and then fill with stuffing. Sprinkle the tops of the mushrooms with Parmesan cheese. Add just enough Sauterne to cover the bottom of the baking dish and bake in a preheated 375° oven for 20 minutes. Serve hot.

Makes 24

STUFFED MUSHROOMS

24 large mushrooms
½ cup chopped parsley
½ cup chopped green onions
½ teaspoon thyme
½ cup butter or margarine
16 slices bacon, cooked and
crumbled
6 ounces cream cheese,
softened
2 cups shredded Cheddar
cheese
melted butter

Remove and finely chop mushroom stems. In a medium-size skillet sauté chopped stems, parsley, green onions and thyme in the ½ cup butter. In a bowl combine bacon, cream cheese and Cheddar cheese. Add the sautéed mixture and stir well. Brush the mushroom caps on both sides with melted butter. Arrange mushrooms hollow side up in an ovenproof dish. Fill mushroom caps with the stuffing. Broil 5 minutes or until cheese is melted.

Makes 24

OYSTERS ROCKEFELLER

If you use a food processor instead of a blender, be careful not to liquefy the greens. The dressing mixture can be made ahead of time and refrigerated. Your local seafood merchant will shuck the oysters for you if you are short on time.

1   cup fresh spinach, stems removed
1   cup minced parsley
1   cup minced green onion tops
4   tablespoons freshly grated Parmesan cheese
⅔   cup unseasoned bread crumbs
1   teaspoon salt
½   teaspoon pepper
¼   teaspoon garlic salt
1   cup butter, melted
12   drops Tabasco
     rock salt
3   dozen half-shells
3   dozen fresh oysters

Combine spinach, parsley and onion tops in a blender. Turn on low speed, gently pushing down greens with wooden spoon until puréed. Set aside. Using an electric mixer combine Parmesan cheese, bread crumbs, salt, pepper, garlic salt, melted butter and Tabasco. Beat for 30 seconds. Add puréed greens and mix well. Spread rock salt evenly over the bottom of a broiler pan. Arrange empty half shells in the salt and place an oyster in each shell. Bake in a preheated 400° oven for 5 minutes. Remove. Put a teaspoon of stuffing on top of each oyster and return to oven for 5 to 8 minutes.

Makes 3 dozen

Have fun matching the decor to your menu. For example, try a nautical motif for seafood. Use blue napkins that have been tied with twine in a sailor's knot. The rest is up to your imagination.

DOLMA

1	16-ounce jar grape leaves
1	pound lean ground lamb
½	cup chopped onions
1	teaspoon chopped mint leaves
¼	cup olive or vegetable oil
1¼	cups long-grain rice
1	tablespoon minced parsley
1	cup plain yogurt
	salt
	pepper
¾	cup lemon juice

Wash grape leaves in cold water. In a large mixing bowl combine the lamb, onions, mint leaves, oil, rice, parsley, yogurt, salt, pepper and ½ cup of the lemon juice. Mix well. Place leaves on a flat surface and cut off excess stems. Place one tablespoon of filling across the top of each leaf. Fold sides over and roll the leaf tightly from one end to the other. When all leaves have been stuffed arrange closely together in a 4 or 5-quart saucepan. Cover with a plate to weigh leaves down and add one inch of water to pan. Cover saucepan tightly and cook over medium heat for 30 minutes. Remove plate and add the remaining ¼ cup of lemon juice. Replace plate and saucepan lid and cook for an additional 15 minutes. May be served warm or cold.

Makes 110

ORIENTAL CHICKEN WINGS

½	cup soy sauce
½	cup brown sugar
¼	cup Mirin (sweet rice wine)
¼	cup peanut oil
1	tablespoon sesame oil
1	garlic clove, minced
1	slice ginger root, peeled and minced
3	green onions, minced
¼	teaspoon pepper
	dash Tabasco
2	tablespoons sesame seeds
2 - 3	pounds chicken wings

Cut off and discard tips of chicken wings. Snip wings in half at the joint. In a 9 × 13-inch ovenproof dish combine all remaining ingredients and blend well. Marinate chicken wings in this mixture overnight turning occasionally. Bake the chicken with its marinade in a preheated 350° oven for 1 hour. Baste several times during cooking.

Makes 36

FUN IN THE SUN BREAK

Chutney Cheese Ball

Assorted Crackers and Breads

Fresh Fruit

Gamay Beaujolais

This lush, tropical backyard is a sharp contrast to the desert in which we live. Waterfalls cascade into the pool, and the rock island provides a delightful spot for snacking during the hot summer months.

ANNA'S SPINACH PIE

One of the charms of this recipe is that it can be assembled several hours before baking if well covered and refrigerated. We usually serve this as an appetizer, but with the addition of a fresh fruit salad, it makes a wonderful summer luncheon.

2	tablespoons olive oil
1	cup chopped green onion
2	garlic cloves, minced
2	shallots, minced
1	10-ounce package frozen chopped spinach, thawed and well drained
8	ounces ricotta cheese
8	ounces feta cheese, crumbled
½	cup freshly grated Parmesan cheese
2	eggs, beaten
1	teaspoon oregano
¼	teaspoon nutmeg
¼	teaspoon pepper
½	cup bread crumbs
½	cup minced parsley
½	pound phyllo dough
1	cup butter or margarine, melted

In a medium-size skillet heat oil and sauté onions, garlic and shallots until soft. Do not brown. Add spinach and cook stirring 1 minute. Remove mixture from heat and place in a large bowl. Add cheeses, eggs, oregano, nutmeg, pepper, bread crumbs and parsley. Mix well and set aside. Lay phyllo dough flat and cover with a damp towel to prevent drying. Lightly brush an 11 × 14-inch baking dish with butter. One at a time, place 6 to 7 layers of phyllo dough in the dish brushing each layer with butter. Gently spread the cheese-spinach mixture over layered dough. Top with another 6 to 7 layers of phyllo dough, again brushing each layer with butter. Bake in a preheated 350° oven 35 minutes or until golden brown. Let stand 5 minutes. Cut into squares to serve.

Serves 12

Clever invitations set the mood for your party no matter what the occasion. For a bon voyage party, write invitations on 3 × 5-inch paper baggage tags. For a New Year's Eve party, enclose a ribbon tied bag of confetti announcing the day and time. For a birthday party, enclose a photograph of the honoree at an earlier birthday with the invitation.

RED HOT PUNCH

This is a festive and colorful punch to serve at family celebrations.

1   cup warm water
1½ cups plus 2 tablespoons
     cinnamon red hot candies
½   cup sugar
2   46-ounce cans pineapple
     juice, chilled
2   quarts ginger ale, chilled
1   quart vanilla ice cream

In a small saucepan combine water, red hots and sugar. Cook over low heat stirring frequently until red hots have melted (approximately 20 to 30 minutes). Strain and allow to cool. In a punch bowl combine red hot mixture with pineapple juice and ginger ale. Just before serving add scoops of ice cream.

Serves 20

WARM AND SPICY AUTUMN PUNCH

2   oranges
     cloves
6   cups apple juice or cider
1   cinnamon stick
¼   teaspoon nutmeg
¼   cup honey
3   tablespoons lemon juice
2¼ cups pineapple juice

Stud the whole oranges with cloves and bake in a preheated 350° oven for 30 minutes. Remove. In a large saucepan combine the apple juice and cinnamon stick. Bring to a boil, reduce heat and simmer 5 minutes. Remove from heat and stir in the nutmeg, honey, lemon juice and pineapple juice. Serve in a punch bowl with whole baked oranges floating on top.

Serves 16

FROZEN FRUIT CRUSH

For extra pizazz substitute chilled Champagne or white wine for half of the ginger ale.

3   cups water
2   cups sugar
1   46-ounce can pineapple juice
1½ cups orange juice
¼   cup lemon juice
3   ripe bananas, mashed
3   quarts ginger ale, chilled

In a 5-quart saucepan combine water and sugar and bring to a boil. Remove from heat and stir in fruit juices and mashed bananas. Pour into 4 ice cube trays or equal size containers and freeze until firm. Remove trays from freezer and let stand 15 to 30 minutes. In a punch bowl break the fruit crush into small chunks and pour ginger ale over all.

Serves 24

STRAWBERRY ROSATO

For an imposing presentation we suggest placing the punch bowl on a large tray and surrounding it with mounds of fresh, ripe strawberries.

4   12-ounce packages frozen sliced strawberries, thawed
1   cup sugar
4   (750 ml) bottles rosé wine, chilled
2   6-ounce cans frozen orange juice concentrate, thawed
2   quarts club soda, chilled

In a large container combine strawberries, sugar and one bottle of wine. Cover and let stand 1 hour. Strain the mixture into a punch bowl and discard strawberries. Add orange juice and stir well. To serve add the remaining 3 bottles of wine and club soda. Stir only slightly.

Makes 6 quarts

CASSIS CHAMPAGNE WITH RASPBERRY CUBES

If you are looking for something extra special, this beverage will lend itself nicely not only in flavor, but presentation.

2   10-ounce packages frozen raspberries in syrup, defrosted and strained to remove seeds
1   cup water
8   tablespoons crème de cassis, chilled
2   (750 ml) bottles Champagne, chilled

To make raspberry ice cubes place strained raspberries and syrup in a bowl. Gently stir in water. Spoon mixture into ice cube trays and freeze until firm. To make individual drinks, pour 1 tablespoon crème de cassis in the bottom of 8 Champagne glasses. Fill glasses with Champagne and float a raspberry cube in each glass. To serve as a punch, combine all ingredients in a large glass bowl.

Serves 8

CHAMPAGNE PUNCH

One thing that says "party" better than any other single offering to your guests is a lovely punch bowl bubbling with a refreshing libation. We think our Champagne Punch is just the ticket for your party.

2   quarts pineapple juice, chilled
2   quarts cranberry juice, chilled
1   12-ounce can frozen orange juice concentrate, thawed
2   cups brandy, chilled
2   quarts 7-Up, chilled
3   magnums Champagne, chilled
    pineapple or rainbow sherbet

Combine juices in a punch bowl. Stir in brandy, 7-Up and Champagne. Float scoops of sherbet in punch.

Serves 15 to 20

WINNEMUCCA MOCHA

1 gallon hot strong coffee
2 cups sugar
2 cups rum, chilled
2 cups milk
1 gallon vanilla ice cream

Combine hot coffee and sugar. Stir and let cool. Add rum and milk. Serve from a punch bowl with scoops of ice cream floating on top.

Serves 40

APRICOT DAIQUIRI

With love and care apricot trees have adapted very well to our semi-arid climate. This recipe is the way its contributor celebrates the bounty of the apricot season.

1 6-ounce can frozen lemonade concentrate
6 ounces rum
6 ripe apricots, peeled and pitted
ice cubes

Combine all ingredients in the container of a blender and add just enough ice cubes to fill it ¾ full. Blend on high until smooth.

Serves 6

PEACH FUZZ

Double or triple this recipe when peaches are at their season's best. The peach mixture freezes beautifully for months — always on hand for a special occasion.

3 large ripe peaches, peeled and pitted
¾ cup sugar
1 6-ounce can frozen lemonade concentrate
10 ounces rum or vodka
ice cubes

Cut peaches into chunks. Place peaches, sugar, frozen lemonade and liquor in the blender and blend until smooth. Freeze. When ready to serve combine equal parts of the peach mixture and ice cubes in a blender. Blend until thick and smooth.

Serves 12

TUMBLEWEED TODDY

Our Tumbleweed Toddy is a most versatile "concoction". Serve it as a refreshing beverage; or freeze it and serve as a dessert. We give you the "how to" for both methods.

8   scoops vanilla ice cream
2   ounces Kahlúa
2   ounces crème de cacao

Combine ingredients in a blender. Blend well. As a beverage, serve over crushed ice. To serve as a dessert, pour the mixture into 4 parfait glasses and freeze. Just before serving, drizzle additional Kahlúa or crème de cacao over each parfait.

Serves 4

AFTER DINNER FRAPPÉ

4   ounces Amaretto liqueur
1⅓ ounces Cointreau liqueur
3   cups fresh orange juice
    (approximately 8 oranges)
½   cup half and half
8   ice cubes

Place all ingredients in a blender. Blend until smooth. Pour into the chilled glasses and serve.

Serves 4

SUNSHINE DUCK

Start your day with this quick-to-prepare healthy breakfast treat. For the calorie conscious, it is also good without the sugar. Protein powder is available at health food stores.

1 6-ounce can frozen orange juice concentrate
1 cup milk
¼ cup sugar
½ teaspoon vanilla
1 egg
1 teaspoon protein powder
4 ice cubes

In a blender combine the frozen orange juice, milk, sugar, vanilla, egg and protein powder. Blend until thoroughly mixed. Add ice cubes and liquefy until ice cubes are crushed.

Serves 4

Breads and Brunch

APPLE MUFFINS

1   egg
½   cup milk
4   tablespoons butter or margarine, melted
1   cup peeled and grated tart apples
1½   cups flour
½   cup sugar
½   teaspoon cinnamon
2   teaspoons baking powder
½   teaspoon salt

In a medium-size bowl beat the egg with a fork. Stir in milk, butter and apples. In a separate bowl combine flour, sugar, cinnamon, baking powder and salt. Add to apple mixture stirring just until the flour is moistened. Batter will be lumpy. Pour into 12 greased muffin tins.

TOPPING

⅓   cup brown sugar
⅓   cup finely chopped nuts
½   teaspoon cinnamon

In a small bowl combine brown sugar, nuts and cinnamon. Sprinkle topping evenly over each muffin. Bake in a preheated 350° oven for 20 to 25 minutes.

Makes 12 muffins

For a springtime party, select 10 4-inch potted bedding flowers and place them in a basket. After the occasion, this living centerpiece can be planted in the yard to give you months more pleasure.

ORANGE DELIGHT MUFFINS

Our Whipped Orange Butter is a natural accompaniment to these muffins.

½   cup butter or margarine
½   cup sugar
1   egg
½   cup bran cereal
½   cup orange juice
¼   cup milk
½   cup crushed pineapple, drained
1¾ cups flour
2   teaspoons baking powder
¼   teaspoon baking soda
¼   teaspoon salt

In a large mixing bowl cream butter and sugar. Add egg and mix well. In a separate bowl combine cereal and orange juice. Stir in milk and pineapple. Add the cereal-fruit mixture to the creamed mixture. Beat in the flour, baking powder, baking soda and salt. Fill 12 greased muffin tins ⅔ full and bake in a preheated 400° oven for 20 minutes.

Makes 12 muffins

BREAKFAST CINNAMON MUFFINS

These breakfast treats are like eating popcorn—once you start you can't stop.

½   cup butter or margarine
¾   cup sugar
1   egg
2   cups flour
2   teaspoons baking powder
½   teaspoon salt
½   teaspoon nutmeg
½   teaspoon allspice
¾   cup milk

In a large mixing bowl cream butter, sugar and egg. In a separate bowl combine flour, baking powder, salt, nutmeg and allspice. Add half of the dry ingredients to the creamed mixture with half of the milk. Mix well and repeat. Fill 12 greased muffin tins ⅔ full. Bake in a preheated 350° oven for 25 to 30 minutes.

COATING

½   cup sugar
1   teaspoon cinnamon
½   cup butter or margarine, melted

Combine sugar and cinnamon in a small bowl. Roll hot muffins in melted butter and then in the sugar-cinnamon mixture. Serve warm.

Makes 12 muffins

BLUEBERRY MUFFINS

Not only do these muffins rise dramatically, they are equally as good made with cranberries.

2   cups flour
2   teaspoons baking powder
½   teaspoon salt
½   cup butter or margarine, softened
1   cup sugar
2   large eggs
1   teaspoon vanilla
½   cup milk
2½ cups fresh blueberries (frozen blueberries thawed and drained can be substituted)

Sift together the flour, baking powder and salt. Set aside. In a large mixing bowl, cream the butter and sugar until fluffy. Thoroughly beat in the eggs. Blend in vanilla. Add half of the dry ingredients to the creamed mixture with half of the milk. Mix well and repeat. Add blueberries and mix gently. Grease and flour twelve 2½-inch muffin cups *and* the tops of the tins between the cups. Spoon batter into prepared cups, filling them to the top.

TOPPING

1   tablespoon sugar
¼   teaspoon ground nutmeg

Combine sugar and nutmeg and sprinkle on top of the muffins. Bake in a preheated 375° oven for 25 to 30 minutes. Let muffins cool 20 minutes before removing from muffin tins. Reheat for five minutes in a preheated 350° oven before serving.

Makes 12 muffins

BLUEBERRY BREAKFAST CAKE

Wonderfully moist and quick to make, this blueberry breakfast cake is a nice way to begin your day.

½ cup butter or margarine, softened
¾ cup sugar
1 egg
¾ cup milk
1 teaspoon vanilla
2 cups flour
1 teaspoon salt
2 teaspoons baking powder
1 cup fresh blueberries (canned and drained blueberries may be substituted)

In a mixing bowl, cream together the butter and sugar. Beat in egg. Blend in milk and vanilla. Add flour, salt and baking powder and mix thoroughly. Gently fold in blueberries and pour batter into a buttered 9 × 9-inch pan.

TOPPING

½ cup butter or margarine, melted
¼ cup sugar
1 tablespoon cinnamon

Gently pour the melted butter evenly over the surface of the batter. Combine sugar and cinnamon and sprinkle over the batter. Bake in a preheated 375° oven for 25 to 30 minutes.

Serves 6

BANANA-MACADAMIA NUT BREAD

½ cup butter or margarine
1 cup sugar
2 eggs
1½ cups flour
1 teaspoon baking soda
½ teaspoon salt
½ cup ground macadamia nuts
1 cup mashed ripe bananas
½ cup chopped walnuts
½ cup chopped macadamia nuts

In a mixing bowl cream together butter and sugar until light and fluffy. Beat in eggs. Sift together flour, soda and salt. Using a fork, mix the ground macadamia nuts into the sifted flour mixture. Add the flour mixture to the butter-sugar mixture, blending well. Stir in mashed bananas, walnuts and chopped macadamia nuts. Spoon the batter into a buttered loaf pan. Bake in a preheated 350° oven for 60 to 70 minutes. Cool 5 minutes, then turn out on a wire rack.

Makes 1 loaf

GRANDMA LOIS' FAMOUS CINNAMON ROLLS

1   package active dry yeast
½   cup lukewarm water
      (110°-115°)
1   tablespoon salt
¼   cup sugar
¼   cup vegetable oil
2   cups water
1   egg
6-6½ cups sifted flour

Dissolve yeast in the ½ cup lukewarm water. When yeast has dissolved, add the salt and sugar. In a large bowl combine oil, water, egg and the yeast-sugar mixture. Slowly add 6 cups of the sifted flour stirring until the dough is smooth and can be gathered into a ball. Place the ball on a lightly floured surface and knead, working in more flour if necessary to make a smooth, elastic, but almost wet dough. Knead dough for 8 to 10 minutes. Place in a greased ceramic or glass bowl, cover and let rise until double in bulk.

ASSEMBLY

½   cup butter, softened
½   cup sugar
1-2 teaspoons cinnamon
6-8 tablespoons butter, melted

Punch dough down and roll on a floured surface into a rectangle approximately 12 × 20-inches. The dough will be sticky, but it should be! Spread the ½ cup softened butter over the top side of the dough. Combine sugar and cinnamon and sprinkle over the butter. Beginning with the long end of the rectangle, roll the dough in jelly-roll fashion and pinch to seal edges. Cut into approximately 1½-inch slices. Put melted butter in an 11 × 15-inch pan (with sides). Place the dough slices in the pan, turning once to coat both sides with the melted butter. Cover rolls and let rise until double in bulk, about 2 hours. Bake in a preheated 375° oven 10 to 15 minutes.

(continued on next page)

BUTTERCREAM FROSTING

2   cups powdered sugar
4   tablespoons butter, softened
1   teaspoon vanilla
¼   cup heavy cream

In a mixing bowl cream powdered sugar with butter. Add vanilla and cream beating to a smooth consistency. Drizzle some of the frosting over the rolls 5 minutes after removing from the oven. Spread the remaining frosting over the rolls after they have cooled. Enjoy!

Makes 12 large rolls

LEMON COFFEE CAKE

1   lemon
½   cup butter
1   cup sugar
2   eggs
½   cup milk
1   teaspoon baking powder
½   teaspoon salt
1¼   cups flour
¼   cup powdered sugar

Grate the rind of the lemon and set aside. Squeeze the lemon and reserve the juice for the glaze. In a large bowl cream the butter and sugar. Beat in the eggs and milk. Sift together the baking powder, salt and flour. Add to the creamed mixture. Stir in the grated lemon peel. Pour the batter into a greased loaf pan. Bake in a preheated 350° oven for 45 minutes. To prepare the glaze blend the powdered sugar with the reserved lemon juice until smooth. When the cake is removed from the oven, poke small holes in the top with a toothpick. Pour the glaze over the hot cake.

Serves 8

JULE'S NUT BREAD

Over one hundred years old, this recipe was brought to America from Germany by the contributor's great-grandmother. It is just as delectable now as it was then.

PASTRY

3	packages active dry yeast
1	teaspoon sugar
1	teaspoon flour
¼	cup lukewarm water (110° - 115°)

In a small bowl combine yeast, sugar, flour and lukewarm water. Set aside to rise for 30 to 60 minutes.

2	cups butter, softened
1	cup sugar
1	teaspoon salt
3	egg yolks
1	tablespoon vanilla
1	cup evaporated milk (heated to 110°)
6	cups flour

In a large mixing bowl cream butter, sugar, salt, egg yolks and vanilla. Stir in evaporated milk and gradually add 6 cups flour to make a dough. Blend in yeast mixture. Turn dough out on a lightly floured board and knead until smooth and elastic. Place dough in a greased bowl, turning to coat entire surface. Cover with a damp cloth and allow to rise until double in bulk (approximately 1 to 3 hours).

NUT FILLING

2	pounds walnuts, ground
2	cups sugar
1	teaspoon vanilla
2	egg whites
1	cup milk (approximately)

Combine nuts, sugar, vanilla and egg whites in a medium-size bowl. Add just enough milk so that mixture will spread smoothly over dough. Cover and set aside.

(continued on next page)

ASSEMBLY

sugar
flour
1 egg, beaten

Divide dough into 6 equal size balls. Using a mixture of half sugar and half flour lightly dust a bread board. With a rolling pin, roll each ball into a 12-inch circle. Spread with nut mixture to within ¼-inch of the edges. Beginning at one side, roll dough into a loaf. Seal ends and place seam side down on a greased cookie sheet (allow 2 loaves per cookie sheet). Make "V" shaped slits across the top of the loaf about ½-inch apart. When all 6 loaves have been filled and shaped, brush the tops of each loaf with beaten egg. Bake in a preheated 350° oven for 35 to 40 minutes.

Makes 6 loaves

SOUR CREAM PECAN COFFEE CAKE

FILLING
1 cup chopped pecans
1 teaspoon cinnamon
2 teaspoons sugar

Combine nuts, cinnamon and sugar. Set aside.

BATTER
1 cup butter, softened
2 cups sugar
2 eggs
1 cup sour cream
½ teaspoon vanilla
2 cups flour
1 teaspoon baking powder
¼ teaspoon salt
powdered sugar

In a large mixing bowl cream butter and sugar until light and fluffy. Beat in eggs one at a time. Blend in sour cream and vanilla on lowest speed of mixer. Sift together the flour, baking powder and salt. Add to the creamed mixture and blend well. Put about ⅓ of the batter into a greased and lightly floured bundt pan. Sprinkle with ¾ of the nut mixture. Spread the remaining batter over the nuts and sprinkle remaining nut mixture over all. Bake in a preheated 350° oven for 60 minutes. Cool on rack for 15 minutes and then turn cake out of pan. Sift powdered sugar over cake after it has completely cooled.

Serves 12

CARDAMOM ORANGE BRAID

For a special treat, offer our Whipped Orange Butter to spread on this flavorful bread.

2	packages active dry yeast
5-6	cups flour
½	teaspoon ground cardamom
1	cup milk
½	cup sugar
1	teaspoon salt
½	cup butter or margarine
1½	tablespoons grated orange rind
⅓	cup orange juice
2	eggs

In a large mixing bowl combine yeast, 2 cups flour and cardamom. In a 1-quart saucepan heat milk, sugar, salt and butter to a temperature of 110° to 115° on a candy thermometer. Stir to melt butter. Add the milk mixture to the dry ingredients beating on low speed with an electric mixer until blended. Add orange rind, juice and eggs. Continue beating on low speed 30 seconds, then increase mixer speed to high and beat an additional 3 minutes. By hand (unless you have a heavy duty mixer) add 3 more cups of flour and mix well. Turn out onto floured board and work in another ½ cup flour. Knead 5 to 8 minutes until smooth and elastic. Put in a greased bowl, turning dough to grease all sides. Cover with a damp cloth and let rise in a warm place until double in bulk (about 1 hour). Punch dough down and divide into six equal size balls. Cover and let rest for 10 minutes. Roll each ball into a rope about 18 to 20-inches in length. To form each loaf, take 3 ropes of dough and braid, pinching ends securely. Do this on a well-greased baking sheet. Cover and let rise 30 minutes more.

1	egg yolk, beaten
1	tablespoon milk

Whisk together egg yolk and milk. Just before baking, brush with the egg yolk-milk mixture. Bake in a preheated 350° oven 20 to 30 minutes or until golden. Serve with orange butter.

Makes 2 loaves

WHIPPED ORANGE BUTTER

½ cup butter, softened
2 tablespoons orange juice concentrate
2 tablespoons powdered sugar
1½ tablespoons finely grated orange rind

Combine all ingredients in a food processor. Process until smooth. Remove the butter mixture to a small serving bowl and chill until ready to serve.

Makes ¾ cup

WHOLE WHEAT MOLASSES BREAD

There is nothing more warming on a chilly day than the lingering aroma of freshly baked bread.

2¾ cups whole wheat flour
1½-2 cups unbleached flour
2 packages active dry yeast
2 tablespoons caraway seeds
1¾ cups water
½ cup dark molasses
¼ cup packed brown sugar
2 tablespoons vegetable shortening
1 tablespoon salt

In a large mixing bowl combine whole wheat flour, 1 cup unbleached flour, yeast and caraway seeds. In a saucepan heat water, molasses, brown sugar, shortening and salt until lukewarm (110° - 115°). Add to dry ingredients and with an electric mixer beat on low speed for ½ minute. Beat on high speed 3 minutes. By hand stir in enough of the remaining unbleached flour to make a stiff dough. Turn dough out onto a well floured board and knead 5 to 8 minutes or until dough is smooth and elastic. Shape into ball. Place in a greased bowl turning once. Cover and let rise until double in bulk (about 1½ hours). Punch dough down and divide in half. Cover and let rest 10 minutes. Shape into 2 loaves and place in greased loaf pans. Cover and let rise 45 minutes. Bake in a preheated 375° oven for 30 to 35 minutes or until bread tests done. Cool on wire rack.

Makes 2 loaves

WHOLE WHEAT BREAD

Surprisingly, you do not need a heavy duty mixer to make this wonderful bread. Because of its volume the contributor of this recipe lets her dough rise in a plastic garbage bag. Yes, that's what she said—a garbage bag. Liquid lecithin and gluten flour are available at health food stores.

3	packages active dry yeast
¾	cup lukewarm water (110° to 115°)
1	teaspoon sugar
1	cup vegetable oil
1	cup honey
3	tablespoons salt
3	tablespoons liquid lecithin
¾	cup gluten flour
7½	cups warm water
20	cups whole wheat flour
1	12-ounce box pitted prunes, stewed and puréed
2-3	tablespoons vegetable oil
½	cup butter, melted

Combine yeast, warm water and sugar. Set mixture aside to double in size. In a large heavy duty mixer combine the oil, honey, salt, lecithin, gluten flour and water. With machine still running, slowly blend in 10 cups whole wheat flour, then add the yeast mixture. Blend in 5 more cups of whole wheat flour and mix for 5 minutes. Add the prunes. Blend in 3 more cups whole wheat flour and finally add more whole wheat flour (approximately 2 cups) until the dough pulls away from the sides of the bowl. Mix 5 minutes longer. Place the dough in a large container which has been coated with 2 to 3 tablespoons of oil. Turn dough over to coat entire surface. Cover and let rise 1½ hours or until double in bulk. Punch down. Separate into 6 to 8 loaves. Place into greased loaf pans. Cover and let rise again for 1 hour or until double in bulk. Bake in a preheated 350° oven for 50 to 60 minutes. Remove from the oven and brush the tops with melted butter. Remove from pans and cool on racks.

THE FOLLOWING DIRECTIONS ARE FOR THE BAKER WHO DOES NOT HAVE A HEAVY DUTY MIXER

Dissolve yeast following the above directions. In a very large mixing bowl combine oil, honey, salt, lecithin, gluten flour and water. By hand mix well. Pour into approximately a 3-gallon container. Add 10 cups of whole wheat flour. Blend. Add yeast mixture. Add 5 more cups of flour and the prunes. Add the remaining flour and knead by hand. Knead until the dough feels elastic, about 10 to 15 minutes. Follow the instructions in the above recipe for rising and baking.

Makes 6 to 8 loaves

CHAMPAGNE BRUNCH PAR EXCELLENCE

Sausage Mushroom Quiche

Shrimp and Artichoke Casserole

Huevos Rancheros for a Crowd

Broccoli Tomato Salad   Cold Armenian Salad

Cardamom Orange Braid   Blueberry Muffins

Roly Poly Strawberry Crepes

Great Grandmother Nazer's German Peach Plum Cake

Luscious Lemon Tarts

Champagne   Coffee

The Desert Inn's 18 hole championship golf course provides a magnificent setting for this champagne brunch. It is the home of the Ladies Professional Golf Association's J & B Scotch Pro Am and is one of four participating courses in the Professional Golf Association's Panasonic Las Vegas Invitational.

Tableware courtesy of Goldwaters Department Store

BRAN BREAD

This luncheon tea bread would be a great accompaniment to our Fabulous Fresh Fruit Salad. Testers also commented that it was wonderful toasted.

3	cups whole wheat flour
2	cups buttermilk
¼	cup honey
¼	cup unprocessed bran
1	tablespoon baking soda
½	cup chopped nuts
½	cup raisins

In a large bowl combine flour, buttermilk, honey, bran and baking soda. Stir well. Add nuts and raisins. Pour the batter into a greased loaf pan. Bake in a preheated 350° oven for 40 to 45 minutes.

Makes 1 loaf

BEST BANANA BREAD

What takes this banana bread out of the realm of "traditional" is the addition of flaked coconut and raisins to the batter.

2	cups flour
1	cup sugar
2	teaspoons cinnamon
2	teaspoons baking soda
1	teaspoon salt
1	cup vegetable oil
2	cups mashed ripe bananas
½	cup raisins
½	cup flaked coconut
3	eggs

In a large bowl sift together the flour, sugar, cinnamon, baking soda and salt. Add the oil, bananas, raisins, coconut and eggs. Mix well. Pour into 2 greased loaf pans and let stand 20 minutes. Bake in a preheated 350° oven for 1 hour or until a toothpick inserted in the center comes out clean.

Makes 2 loaves

Enjoy the bounties of summer. Ask good friends to join you for lunch and have each bring a cup of fresh fruit of their choosing. Toss fruits together in a large crystal bowl. (You will be amazed at the variety.) To complete the fare, offer an assortment of sliced tea breads and refreshing beverages.

CREAM CHEESE AND JAM DANISH LOAVES

This is a refrigerator dough and must chill overnight. The pastry is very impressive when finished and truly worth the effort to prepare.

2   packages active dry yeast
½   cup lukewarm water
     (110°-115°)
     pinch of sugar
¾   cup milk
½   cup butter
½   cup sugar
1½   teaspoons salt
5-5½ cups flour
3   eggs, beaten

In a large mixing bowl dissolve yeast in lukewarm water with a pinch of sugar. In a small saucepan combine milk, butter, sugar and salt. Heat until butter has just melted. Add 2 cups of flour, milk mixture and beaten eggs to yeast. Beat to blend. Beat in 3 more cups of flour. If necessary gradually blend in another ½ cup of flour to make a stiff dough. Turn dough out on a floured board and knead until dough is elastic, about 8 to 10 minutes. Place in a greased bowl turning once. Cover and let rise until double in bulk. Divide dough into thirds and place each third in the center of a greased baking sheet. Roll dough into 9 × 14-inch rectangles.

FILLING

24   ounces cream cheese,
     softened
1½   cups sugar
3   tablespoons fresh lemon juice

Combine cream cheese, sugar and lemon juice in a mixing bowl and beat until smooth. Divide filling into three equal parts and spread down the center (the long way) of each rectangle of dough. Then, on either side of the filling, beginning at the outside edge of the dough, make 3-inch long horizontal cuts through the dough at 1-inch intervals. Fold each strip on the diagonal toward the center of the pastry and over the filling, making a laced effect. Cover and refrigerate overnight. Keep each loaf chilled until ready to bake. Bake individually in a preheated 350° oven for 20 minutes.

(continued on next page)

TOPPING

¾ cup cherry preserves

Remove from oven and spoon ¼ cup cherry preserves down the center of each loaf. Return to oven and bake an additional 5 minutes. Cool completely before frosting.

FROSTING

2¼ cups powdered sugar, sifted
2 tablespoons water
2 tablespoons light corn syrup
1 teaspoon vanilla
¼ teaspoon almond extract

Combine all ingredients in the top of a double boiler. Heat mixture stirring constantly until lukewarm. Do not overheat or the icing will become dull. Remove from heat, but leave over the hot water to keep thin. Using a large wooden spoon, drizzle equal amounts of icing over the three loaves.

Makes 3 loaves

IRISH SODA BREAD

Don't let a St. Patrick's Day go by without making our Irish Soda Bread.

4 cups flour
1½ teaspoons baking soda
1 teaspoon salt
2 tablespoons sugar
¾ cup butter or margarine
1½ cups raisins
1⅓ cups buttermilk
  milk

Sift the flour, baking soda, salt and sugar into a large bowl. Divide the butter into 12 pieces and add to the flour mixture. Using a pastry blender or two knives, cut the butter into the flour mixture until it resembles cornmeal. Stir in raisins. Gradually stir in the buttermilk. (If the mixture seems too dry, add a little more buttermilk.) Knead the dough briefly on a floured surface and form into two round loaves. Place loaves on a greased cookie sheet and with a knife cut a shallow cross on top of each and brush with milk. Bake in a preheated 375° oven for 40 to 50 minutes. The bread is done when it is nicely brown and sounds hollow when tapped. Best when served warm.

Makes 2 loaves

YOU WON'T BELIEVE IT WAFFLES

1   cup sifted flour
2   teaspoons baking powder
1   teaspoon baking soda
1   teaspoon sugar
½   teaspoon salt
1   cup yellow cornmeal
2   eggs, separated
2   cups buttermilk
½   cup vegetable oil

In a large bowl combine flour, baking powder, baking soda, sugar and salt. Stir in the cornmeal. Beat egg yolks and mix with buttermilk and oil; add to the dry ingredients stirring well. Beat egg whites until stiff and fold into the batter. Pour manufacturer's recommended amount of batter into a preheated waffle iron and cook until golden.

Serves 4

OVEN BAKED PANCAKES

A unique Sunday Breakfast treat for the whole family.

6   tablespoons butter or margarine
6   eggs
1   cup flour
1   cup milk
½   teaspoon salt
    powdered sugar
    jelly
    fresh fruit

Melt butter and divide equally among 4 round layer-cake pans. In a bowl combine eggs, flour, milk and salt. Beat well. Divide the batter among the four pans and bake in a preheated 450° oven for 15 minutes. To serve, remove the pancakes from the pans allowing one pancake per person. Serve with powdered sugar, jelly or fresh fruit.

Serves 4

GERMAN PANCAKE WITH THREE FILLINGS

You can easily serve 12 brunch guests by tripling the batter recipe and preparing all three of the fillings.

BATTER

4	tablespoons butter or margarine
1½	cups milk
¾	cup flour
3	eggs
⅓	cup sugar
¼	teaspoon salt

In a 9-inch glass pie plate melt butter in a preheated 400° oven for five minutes. While butter is melting, combine milk, flour, eggs, sugar and salt in a blender. Mix on medium speed until smooth. Remove pie plate from oven and increase oven temperature to 450°. Pour batter into pie plate all at once. Return the plate to the oven and bake for 20 minutes. Reduce oven temperature to 350° and bake an additional 8 to 10 minutes. A well will form in the middle. Serve with one of the following fillings.

STRAWBERRY FILLING

3	cups fresh strawberries, halved
2	tablespoons sugar
1	cup sour cream
¼	cup brown sugar

Sprinkle the strawberries with 2 tablespoons of sugar. Spoon into the center of the hot pancake, cut into wedges and serve with sour cream and brown sugar on the side.

CINNAMON APPLE FILLING

3	apples, peeled, cored and thinly sliced
1½	teaspoons lemon juice
3	tablespoons brown sugar
½	teaspoon cinnamon
3	tablespoons butter

Toss apple slices with lemon juice. Set aside. Mix brown sugar and cinnamon. In a skillet melt butter over medium heat. Stir in apples and sprinkle with the brown sugar-cinnamon mixture. Simmer 15 to 20 minutes and spoon into well of pancake.

ORANGE-MACADAMIA NUT FILLING

½	cup shredded coconut
1	cup orange marmalade
½	cup small pineapple chunks
2	tablespoons Galliano liqueur
½	cup macadamia nuts, finely chopped

Roast coconut in a preheated 300° oven for approximately 10 to 15 minutes or until lightly brown. Remove from oven and combine with the remaining ingredients. Spoon into well of pancake.

Serves 4

GREAT GRANDMOTHER NAZER'S GERMAN PEACH PLUM CAKE

If you are fortunate enough to have home-canned fruit on hand, it tastes particularly delicious in this recipe.

4   tablespoons butter
½   cup sugar
1   egg
1   teaspoon vanilla
1   cup flour
1   teaspoon baking powder
¼   teaspoon salt
1   16-ounce can sliced peaches, drained
1   16-ounce can sliced plums, drained (peeled and pitted if necessary)

In a large mixing bowl cream together butter, sugar, egg and vanilla. Sift together flour, baking powder and salt. Add flour mixture to creamed mixture to form a cookie-like dough. Press dough into a 8½-inch square glass baking dish. Arrange peaches and plums evenly over dough.

TOPPING

½   cup sugar
4   tablespoons butter or margarine
3   tablespoons flour
1   teaspoon cinnamon

Combine sugar, butter, flour and cinnamon. Mix well with a fork until crumbly. Sprinkle on top of fruit. Bake cake in a preheated 350° oven for 30 to 40 minutes. Serve warm.

Serves 6 to 8

CHRISTY'S CREPES

A blender may be used for combining the ingredients for these light, thin crepes.

2 cups flour
¼ teaspoon salt
2 cups cold water
4 eggs
1 tablespoon oil
1 tablespoon butter, melted
  softened butter

In a mixing bowl sift together the flour and salt. Slowly add the water beating with a wooden spoon to prevent lumps. One at a time add the eggs using a wire whisk to blend thoroughly. Add oil and melted butter and continue to whisk until mixture is smooth. Preheat crepe pan and brush with the softened butter. Ladle approximately 2 tablespoons batter into the pan. Tip pan quickly to spread batter evenly over the surface. Brown lightly and then turn with spatula to brown other side. Stack cooked crepes between foil squares. Keep warm if using immediately. To use at a later date, cool crepes, wrap tightly and refrigerate or freeze.

Makes 20 to 24

ROLY POLY STRAWBERRY CREPES

Although we call for strawberries in our Roly Poly Crepes, any fruit or combination of fruits, nuts and raisins may be used for a filling. Kids love Roly Polys because they can eat them on their way out the door.

1 cup flour
3 eggs
1½ cups milk
  dash of salt
  butter
  cinnamon
  sugar
4 cups sliced fresh strawberries

Combine flour, eggs, milk and salt in a blender. Blend on high speed until smooth (about 30 seconds). Scrape down sides and blend another 15 seconds. Refrigerate for at least one hour. To cook the crepes, generously grease a 9-inch sauté pan or griddle. When the pan is hot, ladle 4 tablespoons of batter into the pan. Brown lightly on each side. Remove from pan and slide on to a warm plate. Butter the crepe generously and sprinkle moderately with a mixture of cinnamon and sugar. Add about ⅓ cup of strawberries to each crepe and roll like a jelly roll. Eat immediately.

Makes 12

CREPES BELLISIMO

This entire dish can be prepared a day in advance and refrigerated. Bake just before serving.

16 cooked crepes (see Index)

CREAM SAUCE

4	cups heavy cream
¾	cup freshly grated Parmesan cheese
½	teaspoon salt
⅛	teaspoon white pepper

Bring cream to a boil in a medium-size saucepan. Simmer over low heat 5 minutes. Remove from heat and add cheese, salt and white pepper. Return pan to low heat and stir constantly until cheese is melted. Set aside until ready to fill and assemble.

FILLING

4	tablespoons butter
⅓	cup chopped green onions
1	garlic clove, minced
1	cup finely chopped mushrooms
1	10-ounce package frozen spinach, cooked and drained
2	cups cooked and coarsely chopped turkey or chicken
½	cup cream sauce
1	egg, beaten
⅛	teaspoon pepper
	pinch of nutmeg
½	teaspoon salt

Melt butter in a large skillet. Add green onions and garlic. Cook over medium heat until onions are soft, but not brown. Add mushrooms and cook over medium-high heat until soft. Add spinach and cook over low heat until all liquid has evaporated. Remove from heat and add chicken, ½ cup of the cream sauce, egg, pepper, nutmeg and salt. Stir well and set aside.

ASSEMBLY

	cream sauce
	filling
	crepes
4	tablespoons freshly grated Parmesan cheese

Spread 3 tablespoons of the cream sauce in the bottom of a 9 × 13-inch baking dish. Divide chicken filling evenly among the crepes. Roll up crepes placing seam side down in the baking dish. Pour remaining cream sauce over crepes and sprinkle with Parmesan cheese. Cover and bake in a preheated 350° oven for 15 minutes. Uncover and broil 1 minute if necessary to brown top.

Serves 8

CREPES RANGOON

12 cooked crepes (see Index)

CURRY SAUCE

4   tablespoons butter or margarine
1   medium onion, chopped
½   cup chopped celery
1   small bay leaf, finely crumbled
     pinch of thyme
     salt
     white pepper
1   tablespoon curry powder
2   tablespoons flour
1   cup chicken broth
½   cup heavy cream, room temperature

Melt butter in a skillet and sauté onion and celery until soft. Add bay leaf, thyme, salt, pepper and curry powder. Mix well. Cover and simmer about 3 minutes. In a separate bowl whisk flour into chicken broth. Add to the skillet along with the cream and bring to a boil. Cook until slightly thickened. Set aside until ready to fill crepes.

SEAFOOD FILLING

1   pound uncooked seafood (combination of shrimp, crab and fillet of sole)
     curry sauce

Chop seafood and place in a bowl. Add just enough curry sauce to moisten the seafood.

ASSEMBLY

     filling
     crepes
     warm curry sauce
     pomegranate seeds

Divide seafood filling evenly among the crepes. Roll and place seam side down in a buttered 9 × 13-inch ovenproof dish. Bake in a preheated 375° oven for 20 minutes. Cover with warmed curry sauce and sprinkle with pomegranate seeds before serving.

Serves 4 to 6

SAUSAGE MUSHROOM QUICHE

1   10-inch pastry shell, unbaked
¾   pound sweet Italian sausage, casing removed
½   pound small whole fresh mushrooms
½   cup minced parsley
3   eggs
1½ cups half and half
½   cup freshly grated Parmesan cheese

In a large skillet crumble the sausage. Add the mushrooms and cook about 15 minutes, stirring frequently until meat and mushrooms are lightly browned and all the liquid from the mushrooms has evaporated. Remove from heat and drain off excess fat. Add the parsley and set aside. Beat the eggs thoroughly and then gently blend in the half and half and cheese. Combine this mixture with sausage, mushrooms and parsley. Pour into pastry shell. Turn mushrooms stem end down, arranging evenly over the surface of the filling. Bake in a preheated 375° oven 40 to 55 minutes, or until a knife inserted in the center comes out clean.

Serves 8

QUICHETTES

Ever-so-tasty, our bite-size quichettes would make a welcome addition to almost any buffet table.

1   cup butter or margarine, softened
6   ounces cream cheese, softened
2   cups flour
5   slices bacon, cooked and crumbled
2   cups finely shredded Swiss cheese

Mix butter and cream cheese into flour to form a dough. Wrap in plastic wrap and chill overnight. Using greased miniature muffin tins press ½ tablespoon of the dough evenly into the bottom and all the way up the sides of each cup. Even off tops with a knife or rolling pin. Put ¼ teaspoon of bacon in each cup and loosely fill with shredded cheese.

FILLING

7   eggs
1   cup milk
1   cup half and half
    salt
    nutmeg

In a large mixing bowl beat eggs, milk, half and half and seasonings. Blend well. Using a meat baster, fill each cup to the top with the egg mixture. Bake in a preheated 375° oven 15 minutes or until puffed and brown.

Makes 40 to 45

VEGETABLE QUICHE

You can vary the taste and appearance of this quiche by creating your own combination of vegetables.

1   10-inch pastry shell, baked and cooled
2   tablespoons butter or margarine
½   onion, chopped
2   cups chopped vegetables (broccoli, cauliflower, spinach or mushrooms)
1½ cups grated Cheddar or Swiss cheese
1   tablespoon minced parsley
4   strips bacon, cooked and crumbled
3   eggs
½   cup milk

In a large skillet melt butter and sauté onion and chopped vegetables until limp. Spoon into the baked pastry shell. Sprinkle cheese over the vegetables and top with the parsley and crumbled bacon. Whisk together the eggs and milk and pour over the vegetables. Bake in a preheated 400° oven for 15 minutes. Reduce heat to 350° and bake an additional 20 minutes. Let stand 5 minutes before serving.

Serves 6 to 8

SHRIMP AND ARTICHOKE CASSEROLE

6½ tablespoons butter or margarine
4½ tablespoons flour
1   cup heavy cream
½   cup half and half
1   tablespoon Worcestershire sauce
3   tablespoons dry Sherry
1   pound fresh mushrooms, sliced
1   14-ounce can artichoke hearts, drained and quartered
1½ pounds cooked shrimp, shelled and deveined
1   cup freshly grated Parmesan cheese

In a saucepan melt 4½ tablespoons of the butter. Add flour and blend until smooth. Stir in cream and half and half. Cook until thickened. Blend in Worcestershire sauce and Sherry. Set aside. In a large skillet sauté mushrooms in remaining 2 tablespoons butter. Line a 3-quart casserole with the sautéed mushrooms. Arrange artichokes and shrimp evenly over the mushrooms. Pour the sauce over all and bake in a preheated 425° oven for 20 minutes. Remove from oven, sprinkle with cheese, and broil until lightly browned.

Serves 6

SUNRISE BRUNCH

Our Frosted Melon Mold would be the perfect accompaniment to this morning entrée. Important to note is that this dish must be assembled and refrigerated for 24 hours before baking.

butter or margarine, softened
16 slices French bread, crusts removed
1 pound Cheddar cheese, grated
1 pound Monterey Jack cheese, grated
1 pound bacon, cooked and crumbled
1 cup sliced fresh mushrooms
½ cup chopped onion
1 red or green bell pepper, chopped
14 eggs
2 cups half and half
1 teaspoon salt
½ teaspoon pepper
½ teaspoon paprika
½ teaspoon dry mustard

Spread butter on both sides of the bread slices and place half of them in a buttered 9 × 13-inch ovenproof casserole. Sprinkle half of each of the cheeses and half of the bacon over the bread slices. Place the remaining eight slices of bread over all and sprinkle with the remaining cheeses and bacon. Top with mushrooms, onion and bell pepper. In a separate mixing bowl beat eggs, half and half and seasonings. Pour egg mixture over the bread and cheeses. Refrigerate for 24 hours. Bake in a preheated 350° oven for 1½ hours.

Serves 10 to 12

HANGTOWN FRY

This egg dish is great served with a dark bread such as rye or pumpernickel.

1 pint oysters
4 tablespoons butter or margarine
3 tablespoons chopped onions
6 eggs
¼ cup beer
¼ teaspoon salt
¼ teaspoon Tabasco
¼ teaspoon garlic salt
4 slices bacon, cooked and crumbled

Drain oysters and pat dry with a paper towel. In a large heavy skillet melt butter. Sauté onions until transparent. Add oysters and cook just until the edges begin to curl. Remove from heat. In a mixing bowl beat eggs with beer, salt, Tabasco, garlic salt and bacon. Pour egg mixture evenly over oysters. Return to heat and cook on low, stirring constantly, until eggs are scrambled.

Serves 6

SAUSAGE - SPINACH À LA PARMA

1 pound sweet Italian sausage, casing removed
6 eggs, beaten
1 10-ounce package frozen chopped spinach, thawed and drained
1 pound mozzarella cheese, shredded
1 cup ricotta cheese
½ teaspoon salt
⅛ teaspoon pepper
⅛ teaspoon garlic powder
½ cup grated red onion
freshly grated Parmesan cheese

In a skillet over medium heat brown and crumble the sausage. Drain well. Combine the sausage with all remaining ingredients except the Parmesan cheese. Mix well and pour into a buttered 2-quart ovenproof casserole. Sprinkle with the Parmesan cheese and bake in a preheated 350° oven for 45 minutes.

Serves 10 to 12

MUSHROOM QUICHE

1 9-inch pastry shell, unbaked
4 eggs, beaten
½ pound mushrooms, sliced
¼ cup chopped green onion
1 tablespoon butter or margarine
1 cup shredded Swiss cheese
1 cup half and half
¼ cup freshly grated Parmesan cheese
½ teaspoon salt
⅛ teaspoon pepper

Brush the inside of the pastry shell with a small amount of the beaten egg. Prick bottom and sides. Bake in a preheated 450° oven until golden brown (about 5 minutes). Remove from the oven and reduce oven temperature to 375°. In a skillet sauté mushrooms and onion in butter 6 to 8 minutes. Remove from heat and stir in Swiss cheese. Pour into pastry shell. To the beaten eggs, add half and half, Parmesan cheese, salt and pepper. Mix well. Pour over mushroom mixture. Bake 35 to 45 minutes or until a knife inserted in the center comes out clean.

Serves 8

Soups, Salads
and Sandwiches

CHILLED RASPBERRY SOUP

Chilled fruit soups may be appropriately served as a first course, or at the end of the meal, as a dessert soup.

4	cups fresh raspberries, rinsed and drained
½	cup sugar
1¾	cups chilled dry white wine
1	cup water

Reserve 12 raspberries and set aside. Put remaining berries in the container of a food processor or blender. Process 20 seconds or until puréed. Combine puréed raspberries, sugar, wine and water. Mix well and chill. When ready to serve, ladle into individual bowls and float reserved berries on top.

Serves 4

COLD STRAWBERRY SOUP

In the Southwest late March hails the beginning of the strawberry season. Ardent local gardeners cultivate borders of the plant that bears this flavorful fruit. This cold soup is one of the ways we welcome this advent of spring.

1	pound fresh strawberries
1	cup water
1	(750 ml) bottle port wine
4	tablespoons sugar
⅛	teaspoon salt
	juice of 1 lemon
3	tablespoons arrowroot
	sour cream

If the strawberries are large, cut in half. Set aside one whole berry for each individual serving. In a 4-quart saucepan combine remaining berries, water and all but ¼ cup of the wine. Stir in sugar, salt and lemon juice. Simmer for 5 minutes. In a small bowl blend arrowroot with the remaining ¼ cup of wine. Pour into soup stirring well. Bring to the boiling point and remove from heat. Refrigerate until chilled. To serve, pour into individual bowls and garnish with a small amount of sour cream topped with a whole berry.

Serves 6 to 8

CHEESY VEGETABLE SOUP

This hearty and nourishing soup is bound to warm you on a cold winter's eve.

3   cups water
2½ cups chicken broth
2   cups diced celery
2   cups peeled and thinly sliced carrots
2   cups broccoli flowerets
1   cup thinly sliced leek (whites only)
2   tablespoons butter
2   tablespoons flour
2   cups shredded Danish Creamy Havarti cheese
½ cup heavy cream
    dash cayenne
2   egg yolks, beaten

In a large heavy bottomed saucepan combine water and broth. Bring to a boil. Add vegetables and cook over medium heat about 5 to 10 minutes or until barely tender. Strain vegetables and reserve liquid. Set vegetables aside. Return liquid to the saucepan and bring to a boil. In a small bowl blend butter with flour to make a smooth paste and add to boiling liquid. Stir well. Reduce heat and add cheese, cream and cayenne, stirring constantly until smooth. Blend a small amount of hot liquid into beaten egg yolks. Stir egg yolk mixture into soup. Return vegetables to the soup base and heat through. Do not boil or eggs will scramble.

Serves 4 to 6

CREAM OF BROCCOLI SOUP

"Beautiful soup, so rich and green, waiting in a hot tureen." (Lewis Carroll) It's always nice to have a recipe for good traditional broccoli soup on hand.

6   tablespoons butter
2   medium onions, diced
2   stalks celery, diced
2   garlic cloves, minced
3   pounds fresh broccoli
4   cups chicken broth
⅛ teaspoon marjoram
⅛ teaspoon thyme
⅛ teaspoon savory
1   bay leaf
2   cups heavy cream
    salt
    freshly ground pepper
    garlic seasoned croutons

Melt butter in a 4-quart saucepan over low heat. Add onions and celery. Cook until transluscent, about 5 minutes. Add garlic and cook 3 minutes more. Remove broccoli flowerets from stems and set aside. Add stems to saucepan. Blend in chicken broth and herbs. Cover and simmer over low heat for 1 hour. Transfer to blender and purée soup in batches. Return puréed soup to saucepan and stir in cream. Cover partially and simmer for 30 minutes. Add broccoli flowerets and cook until just tender (about 4 to 6 minutes). Season with salt and pepper. Garnish with croutons.

Serves 8 to 10

OLD ENGLISH PEA SOUP

The chervil is a nice addition to this soup.

5 tablespoons butter
1 leek, minced (white only)
½ small onion, minced
½ head Boston lettuce, shredded
1 tablespoon flour
¼ teaspoon ground coriander
¼ teaspoon white pepper
2½ cups fresh or frozen peas
4 cups chicken broth
1 teaspoon sugar
1 cup half and half
  salt
1 teaspoon chopped fresh chervil (or ½ teaspoon dried)

In a Dutch oven melt 3 tablespoons butter and sauté leek, onion and lettuce until lettuce is wilted. Blend in flour and cook for two minutes over low heat. Add coriander, pepper, peas, broth and sugar. Simmer until peas are just tender. Using a slotted spoon remove ½ cup whole peas and reserve. In a blender or food processor, purée remaining vegetables and broth. Return puréed mixture to heat, add cream and season with salt. Heat soup to boiling and swirl in remaining butter. To serve, garnish with reserved whole peas and chervil.

Serves 6 to 8

SCALLOP SOUP

A special dinner calls for an extra special beginning. This scallop soup is an elegant first course.

6 cups chicken broth
¾ pound scallops
2 tablespoons dry Sherry
¼ teaspoon white pepper
1 teaspoon tarragon
3 large green onions, trimmed and sliced diagonally at ⅛-inch intervals
  salt
1½ teaspoons cornstarch
1½ tablespoons cold water

In a 4-quart saucepan bring chicken broth to a boil. Add scallops and immediately reduce heat. Cover and simmer 1 hour. Remove saucepan from heat. With a slotted spoon remove scallops and shred. Return scallops to the soup base. Again bring soup to a simmer and add Sherry, pepper, tarragon, green onions and salt to taste. In a small bowl combine cornstarch with water to make a paste. Whisk into the soup. Adjust seasonings to taste and serve hot.

Serves 6

SAVORY SHRIMP SOUP

½ cup butter
1 tablespoon minced garlic
1 tablespoon minced shallots
1 cup white wine
1 bay leaf
¾ cup Sherry
1 pound diced raw shrimp
2 quarts milk or half and half
1 cup clam juice
6 tablespoons arrowroot or cornstarch
   salt
   white pepper
½ cup diced red pepper

In a heavy 1 gallon stockpot melt 4 tablespoons of the butter. Add garlic and shallots and sauté until lightly brown. Add white wine, bay leaf and ½ cup of the Sherry. In a separate skillet sauté shrimp briefly in remaining 4 tablespoons of butter and add to wine mixture. Stir in milk. Allow soup base to almost reach a boil and then add clam juice. In a small saucepan make a roux with the remaining ¼ cup Sherry and arrowroot. Blend into soup stirring until thickened. Season with salt and pepper. Serve soup in individual bowls and garnish with diced red peppers.

Serves 8

If you are hosting a large patio reception or buffet, why not serve one of our cold fruit soups in long stemmed wine glasses.

SPANISH TRAIL PEA SALAD

This is a terrific salad for toting to a "potluck". It serves a crowd and can be prepared well in advance of festivities.

1   tablespoon prepared horseradish
1   teaspoon dry mustard
1   teaspoon coarsely ground pepper
    dash of seasoned salt
    dash of garlic salt
4   tablespoons sugar
2   tablespoons lemon juice
2   cups sour cream
1   cup mayonnaise
3   16-ounce packages frozen peas, thawed and drained
3   cups Spanish peanuts
2   cups chopped green onions

In a large bowl combine horseradish, dry mustard, pepper, salts, sugar, lemon juice, sour cream and mayonnaise. Mix well. Add the peas, peanuts and onions. Toss lightly and refrigerate at least 1 day before serving.

Serves 25

FROSTED MELON MOLD

Although we created our showy frosted melon mold using raspberries and raspberry jello, you may use any combination of fruit and jello you wish.

1   melon (cantaloupe or honeydew)
1   6-ounce package raspberry jello
1   10-ounce package frozen raspberries, thawed and drained
8   ounces cream cheese, softened
    milk
1   large head lettuce

Peel the entire melon. Cut a slice from the end of the melon and remove seeds with a spoon. Prepare jello following package directions for adding fruit. Add well-drained raspberries. Fill the cavity of the melon with this mixture and refrigerate melon upright until jello is firm. Beat just enough milk into the cream cheese to make the cheese of spreading consistency. Remove melon from refrigerator and frost the entire surface with the cheese. Again, refrigerate melon until frosting is firm. To serve, slice the melon crosswise and arrange slices on a bed of lettuce.

Serves 8

FABULOUS FRESH FRUIT SALAD

Fruit, glorious fruit! We have given you a guideline on quantities and types of fruits, but any combination you create will be just as delectable. Let the season dictate what your basket will bring home for this beautiful refreshing salad. To complete a luncheon fare serve several varieties of our tea breads. Suspend a plump ripe strawberry in a fluted glass of white wine for the perfect apéritif.

2   kiwi, peeled
2   peaches, peeled
2   apples
2   bananas, peeled
1   cup grapes (green or seeded red)
½   cup chopped walnuts
1   cup plain yogurt
¼   cup honey
1   cup blueberries (1 cup frozen blueberries, thawed and well-drained, may be substituted)
    shredded coconut

Slice kiwi, peaches, apples and bananas into a large bowl. Add whole grapes and chopped walnuts and toss. Mix the fresh fruit and nuts with yogurt and honey. Toss again. Just before serving, gently mix in the blueberries, being careful that they do not discolor the salad. Serve in a large glass compote and sprinkle with shredded coconut.

Serves 4 to 6

ORIENTAL CHICKEN SALAD

Rice sticks are an oriental product. They fry and expand very quickly.

2   tablespoons slivered almonds
2   tablespoons sesame seeds
3   whole chicken breasts, cooked, skinned, boned and shredded
4   green onions, chopped
2   ounces rice sticks
1   large head lettuce, chopped

DRESSING

½   cup vegetable oil
6   tablespoons cider vinegar
4   tablespoons sugar
1½   teaspoons salt
1   teaspoon pepper

In a preheated 300° oven toast almonds and sesame seeds until lightly browned. In a large bowl toss shredded chicken with the sesame seeds, almonds and onions. Cover and refrigerate. Just before serving fry the rice sticks according to package directions. Add the fried rice sticks and lettuce to the chicken mixture. Toss with dressing.

Combine oil, vinegar, sugar, salt and pepper. Blend well and pour over chicken mixture to taste.

Serves 8

CHICKEN SALAD GOURMET

This salad is particularly attractive garnished with a slice of fresh watermelon or cantaloupe.

½ cup pecan halves
5 cups diced cooked chicken
2 cups diced celery
½ pound whole button mushrooms
4 slices bacon, cooked and crumbled
1 cup mayonnaise
1 cup sour cream
½ teaspoon salt
2 tablespoons lemon juice
1 large head lettuce

Toast pecan halves in a preheated 350° oven for 10 minutes. In a large bowl combine pecans, chicken, celery, mushrooms and bacon. One at a time add mayonnaise, sour cream, salt and lemon juice. Toss well after each addition. Using individual serving plates, arrange salad on a bed of lettuce.

Serves 6

PASTA SALAD

½ cup olive oil
½ cup vegetable oil
juice of 1 lemon
2 garlic cloves, minced
1 cup fresh basil leaves, minced
1 pound small pasta shells
5 ounces thinly sliced pepperoni
1 15½-ounce can garbanzo beans
1 cup cubed Cheddar cheese
1 cup cubed mozzarella cheese
1 cup pitted black olives
½ cup freshly grated Parmesan cheese

In a food processor or blender combine oils, lemon juice, garlic and basil. Process for 20 seconds. Cook pasta al dente and drain well. In a large bowl combine pasta with ⅓ of the dressing. Allow mixture to cool. Add pepperoni, garbanzo beans, cheese and olives. Refrigerate overnight. Just before serving toss with additional dressing and Parmesan cheese.

Serves 6 to 8

CAESAR'S SALAD

Be a star! Entertain guests with your culinary flair by preparing and serving this salad at the table.

⅓ cup vegetable oil
1 garlic clove, mashed
   dash of Worcestershire sauce
1 large head romaine lettuce, torn in bite-size pieces
1 egg, beaten
   juice of ½ lemon
½ cup freshly grated Parmesan cheese
6 anchovy fillets, mashed
½ cup homemade croutons

In a small bowl combine the oil, garlic and Worcestershire sauce. Set aside to allow flavors to blend. Place lettuce in a large salad bowl. To prepare the salad add the following ingredients tossing well after each addition: beaten egg, oil mixture, lemon juice, Parmesan cheese, anchovies and croutons.

Serves 4

HOMEMADE MICROWAVE CROUTONS

2 slices bread, fresh or day old
1½ tablespoons butter

Remove crusts from bread and discard. Cut bread into ½-inch cubes. Place butter in an 8 × 8-inch glass dish and melt in a microwave oven. Remove and stir in bread cubes tossing to coat all sides with melted butter. Return to the microwave and cook on full-power for 1 minute. Stir croutons and cook for an additional 1½ minutes on full-power. (They will not brown.) Croutons will become crisp and crunchy as they cool.

Makes 1 cup

SALAD NIÇOISE

Start to prepare this dressing a day in advance. It will allow the olive oil time to absorb the essence of the garlic.

SALAD DRESSING

2   garlic cloves, crushed
1½ cups olive oil
¼   cup white wine vinegar
1   tablespoon fresh minced
    herbs (1½ teaspoons dried
    herbs may be substituted)

Soak the garlic cloves in the olive oil overnight. The next day add vinegar and any combination of herbs (for example: parsley, oregano, rosemary, basil). Shake well.

SALAD INGREDIENTS

1   head romaine lettuce
2   heads butter lettuce
3   potatoes, peeled, boiled and
    cubed
3   tomatoes, cut in wedges
½   cucumber, thinly sliced
¾   cup whole pitted black olives
4   tablespoons peeled and
    grated carrots
4   tablespoons minced fresh
    parsley
    pepper
4   hard boiled eggs, halved
    lengthwise
8   anchovy fillets
8   artichoke hearts

Wash and dry lettuces. Tear into bite-size pieces. In a large bowl combine lettuces, potatoes, tomatoes, cucumber, olives, 2 tablespoons of the grated carrot and 2 tablespoons of the parsley. Season with pepper. Sparingly add dressing and toss lightly. To serve, sprinkle remaining carrots and parsley on top. Place an anchovy fillet on each egg half. Garnish salad with the egg and artichoke hearts.

Serves 8

HOT POTATO SALAD

All of our testers loved this German-style potato salad. You will too!

5   pounds potatoes, peeled
½   pound bacon, diced
¾   cup sugar
¾   cup water
¾   cup cider vinegar
1   teaspoon dry mustard
2   eggs, beaten
1   small onion, sliced
1   green pepper, diced
    salt
    pepper
3   hard boiled eggs, sliced
    (optional)

Boil potatoes until fork-tender. Cool and slice. In a large skillet fry bacon until crisp. Remove bacon from skillet and drain well. To the pan drippings add sugar, water, vinegar, mustard and the beaten egg. Cook for about 3 minutes stirring constantly. In a large bowl combine the sliced potatoes, bacon, onion and green pepper. Pour the hot dressing over the vegetables and toss. Season with salt and pepper. Add hard boiled eggs if desired. Serve warm.

Serves 8

COLD ARMENIAN SALAD

You don't have to be a vegetarian or a health food fan to enjoy this interesting combination of ingredients.

1   cup fine bulgar (cracked wheat)
¼   cup minced parsley
4   green onions, chopped
3   large tomatoes, chopped
10 tablespoons olive oil
5   tablespoons lemon juice
1   teaspoon allspice
1   teaspoon salt
    pepper

In a bowl combine bulgar, parsley, green onions, and tomatoes. Add the oil and toss. Add the lemon juice and toss again. Blend in the allspice, salt and mix well. Adjust seasonings to taste. Cover salad and refrigerate 3 hours or until wheat has absorbed the liquid.

Serves 8

SUMMER SALAD WITH HOMEMADE MAYONNAISE

2 cups fresh broccoli flowerets
2 cups fresh cauliflower flowerets
¾ cups fresh peas (frozen peas, thawed and drained, may be substituted)
2 green onions, chopped
¾ cup homemade mayonnaise
½ cup sour cream
½ teaspoon minced garlic
¼ teaspoon pepper
   salt to taste
½ cup cooked and crumbled bacon

Toss broccoli, cauliflower, peas and onions with mayonnaise and sour cream. Add seasonings and half of the bacon. Toss again. Garnish with remaining bacon.

Serves 6

HOMEMADE MAYONNAISE

1 egg
½ teaspoon dry mustard
1 tablespoon fresh lemon juice
1 tablespoon vinegar
½ teaspoon salt
1 cup olive oil

Place egg, mustard, lemon juice, vinegar, salt and ¼ cup of olive oil in a blender or food processor. Cover and blend. With machine still on, remove cap and slowly pour in the remaining oil in a steady stream. Process until thoroughly blended. Refrigerate until ready to use.

Makes 1¼ cups

Do something special for your guests (and yourself). Serve soup, salads or ices in fresh fruit shells. We like our "Gourmet Chicken Salad" in a hollowed cantaloupe, or try our "Sure Bet Lemon Sherbet" in an orange shell.

MAY DAY LUNCHEON POOLSIDE

Cold Raspberry Soup

Crepes Bellisimo

Fresh Greens with Walnut Dressing

Mandarin Delight

Iced Tea   Chenin Blanc

This lovely Las Vegas backyard with poolside cabana is ideal for outdoor entertaining. The casually set poolside table is charming for an informal luncheon. Warm spring days in Las Vegas make outdoor entertaining a delight.

Tableware provided by Bullock's Department Store

CACTUS CAVIAR

Don't bypass this salad recipe. It is one of our favorites!

1¼	cups water
16	ounces frozen black eyed peas
2	cups oil and vinegar dressing
2	cups diced green pepper
1½	cups diced onion
1	cup chopped green onions
1	4-ounce can diced green chiles
1	tablespoon minced garlic
1	2-ounce jar chopped pimientos, drained
	salt
1	dash Tabasco

In a medium-size saucepan bring the water to a boil. Add peas and bring to a second boil. Cover and reduce heat to low and cook 15 to 20 minutes. Drain peas. Place the peas in a large bowl and add the oil and vinegar dressing. Let cool. Add remaining ingredients and mix well. Refrigerate for several hours or overnight before serving.

Makes 7½ cups

CHILLED GREEN PEA SALAD

One of our testers exclaimed that "this easy to prepare salad is positively perfect for summer outdoor dining—even when the thermometer hits 100° plus!"

2	10-ounce packages frozen peas
1	bunch green onions, chopped
1½	cups shredded Cheddar cheese
2	stalks celery, chopped
1	cup seasoned croutons
	Ranch style dressing

Cook peas until just fork-tender. Do not overcook. Drain peas and allow to cool. In a bowl combine cooled peas, onions, cheese and celery. Chill. Just before serving add croutons and toss with Ranch style dressing.

Serves 6 to 8

MUSHROOM SALAD

3 cups thinly sliced mushrooms
1 cup diced celery
½ cup diced green pepper
½ red onion, sliced
½ cup diced pimientos
1 cup bean sprouts
2 teaspoons red wine vinegar
1 teaspoon minced garlic
½ teaspoon Worcestershire sauce
½ teaspoon salt
½ cup vegetable oil

In a large bowl combine mushrooms, celery, green pepper, red onion, pimiento and sprouts. In a separate bowl combine vinegar, garlic, Worcestershire and salt. Add oil in a stream, whisking continuously. Toss vegetables with dressing and serve.

Serves 8

MUSHROOM AND SWISS CHEESE SALAD

½ pound fresh mushrooms
  juice of 1 lemon
1 bunch green onions, chopped
⅔ cup julienned Swiss cheese
3 tablespoons olive oil
  salt
  freshly ground black pepper
1 head butter lettuce

Remove stems from mushroom caps and discard. Slice caps, place in a bowl, and sprinkle with lemon juice. Add green onions, cheese and olive oil. Salt and pepper to taste. Toss and serve on beds of butter lettuce.

Serves 4

TOMATOES VINAIGRETTE

We know you will agree that one of the taste treats of summer is to please the palate with vine-ripened tomatoes. Our tangy vinaigrette is all you need to compliment this colorful vegetable.

12   thick tomato slices
1   cup olive oil
⅓   cup red wine vinegar
2   teaspoons crushed oregano
    leaves
1   teaspoon salt
½   teaspoon pepper
½   teaspoon dry mustard
2   garlic cloves, crushed
    lettuce leaves
    minced green onion
    minced parsley

Arrange tomato slices in an 8 × 8-inch dish. In a bowl whisk together the oil, vinegar, oregano, salt, pepper, mustard and garlic. Spoon over tomato slices. Cover and chill at least 2 hours. Occasionally spoon dressing over the tomatoes. To serve, arrange tomatoes on lettuce leaves and sprinkle with a small amount of dressing. Garnish with minced green onion and parsley.

Serves 4 to 6

HONEYMOON SPINACH SALAD

We had several spinach salad recipes submitted for testing. We agreed, this spinach salad beat them all!

½   bunch spinach leaves, stems
    removed
6   strips bacon
¼   cup Parmesan cheese
2   hard boiled eggs, grated
¼   cup diced red onion
1   tablespoon Worcestershire
    sauce
3   tablespoons red wine vinegar

Wash and towel dry spinach leaves. Set aside. Place 2 ovenproof ceramic bowls in a preheated 350° oven until very hot. In a small skillet cook bacon until crisp and crumbly. Drain and reserve ¼ cup bacon grease. Remove bowls from the oven and divide equally between them the spinach leaves, bacon, cheese, eggs, onion, Worcestershire sauce and vinegar. Add the hot bacon grease to each salad, toss and serve.

Serves 2

MARINATED VEGETABLE SALAD

We suggest slicing the zucchini, carrots and celery on the diagonal. This bounty of fresh vegetables is an attractive addition to any buffet table.

2 cups fresh cauliflower
   flowerets
1 zucchini, sliced
2 medium carrots, peeled and
   thinly sliced
1 green pepper, sliced into
   rings
½ pound fresh mushrooms,
   sliced
2 green onions, chopped
2 cups sliced celery
1 6-ounce jar marinated
   artichoke hearts, drained and
   sliced

Combine vegetables in a 9 × 13-inch shallow casserole.

MARINADE

¼ cup vegetable oil
⅓ cup sugar
½ cup cider vinegar
2 tablespoons water

Whisk together the oil, sugar, vinegar and water. Pour over vegetables and refrigerate. Marinate overnight and occasionally spoon marinade over vegetables.

Serves 8

ZUCCHINI SALAD

¼ cup red wine vinegar
⅓ cup olive oil
2 teaspoons garlic salt
¼ teaspoon paprika
¼ teaspoon pepper
¼ teaspoon basil
¼ teaspoon sugar
1 pound zucchini, sliced
1 cup stuffed green olives, sliced in half
1 large avocado, peeled and cubed
   lettuce leaves

In a small bowl whisk together the vinegar, olive oil, garlic salt, paprika, pepper, basil and sugar. Set aside. Steam zucchini until tender but crisp. Place zucchini and olives in a shallow dish and cover with marinade. Marinate at least 6 hours or overnight. Just before serving add cubed avocado and toss lightly. Serve on a bed of lettuce.

Serves 6 to 8

BROCCOLI TOMATO SALAD

For a perfect summer supper serve this salad with a variety of cold sliced meats and French bread.

3 pounds broccoli, cut lengthwise
2 large firm tomatoes, cut in ¾-inch cubes
2 tablespoons chopped red onion
¾ cup mayonnaise
2 teaspoons soy sauce
1½ teaspoons lemon juice
1 teaspoon salt
½ cup slivered almonds
2 hard boiled eggs, chopped
18 pitted ripe black olives

Steam broccoli until tender, 5 to 7 minutes. Rinse with cold water and drain well. Cut into bite-size pieces and place in a large bowl. Add tomatoes and onion, and toss lightly. Refrigerate for at least 2 hours. To prepare dressing combine mayonnaise, soy sauce, lemon juice and salt. Mix well and chill. Just before serving, add almonds, eggs and olives to the broccoli and tomatoes. Toss the salad with the dressing.

Serves 10 to 12

ARTICHOKE SALAD

If refrigerated, the flavors of this salad hold exceptionally well for several days.

2   6-ounce jars marinated
    artichoke hearts
1   cup long-grain rice
2   teaspoons chicken broth
2   green peppers, chopped
1   6½-ounce can sliced water
    chestnuts, drained
8   fresh mushrooms, sliced
½   cup sliced green olives
¼   cup chopped almonds
1   cup mayonnaise
1   teaspoon lemon juice
1   teaspoon curry powder

Drain artichoke hearts and reserve juice. Set aside. Prepare rice according to package directions adding 2 teaspoons chicken broth to the liquid before cooking. Cool cooked rice. In a large bowl combine the cooled rice with the artichoke hearts, chopped peppers, water chestnuts, mushrooms, olives and almonds. In a small bowl whisk together the reserved artichoke juice, mayonnaise, lemon juice and curry powder. Toss with salad ingredients and refrigerate overnight.

Serves 6 to 8

POPPY SEED SALAD DRESSING

This dressing is excellent served over fresh spinach, or a combination of sectioned grapefruit and sliced avocado. One of our testers noted that this recipe for Poppy Seed Dressing is the one she always wished she had, but never did ... until now!

⅓   cup white wine vinegar
⅓   cup honey
2   teaspoons Dijon-style
    mustard
1   teaspoon salt
3   tablespoons chopped onion
1   cup vegetable oil
1½ tablespoons poppy seeds

In a blender or food processor combine vinegar, honey, mustard and salt. Process until smooth. Add chopped onion. With the blender running, gradually add vegetable oil until mixture thickens. Finally, blend in poppy seeds. Refrigerate in an air-tight container until ready to use.

Makes 1½ cups

ANCHOVY AND LIME VINAIGRETTE

Select several varieties of lettuce at your local market. Add sliced fresh mushrooms, homemade croutons and toss with our anchovy flavored vinaigrette. It is bound to please even the most discriminating tastes.

¼ cup olive oil
¾ cup salad oil
1 egg yolk
½ teaspoon Worcestershire
   sauce
1 garlic clove, crushed
1 teaspoon salt
1 teaspoon pepper
1 teaspoon dry mustard
1 teaspoon Dijon-style mustard
2 tablespoons white vinegar
2 tablespoons lime juice
   3-inch ribbon of anchovy
   paste or 3 minced anchovies

Combine all ingredients in a food processor or blender and process for 1 minute. Refrigerate until ready to use.

Makes 1½ cups

WALNUT SALAD DRESSING

3 tablespoons Dijon-style
   mustard
⅓ cup red wine vinegar
½ cup walnut oil
⅓ cup vegetable oil
1 tablespoon minced parsley
2 tablespoons chopped shallots

In a small bowl whisk together the mustard and vinegar. Gradually add the oil and continue to whisk until well combined. Stir in the parsley and shallots. Refrigerate until ready to serve.

Makes 1¼ cups

OPEN-FACE SHRIMP SANDWICH

6   ounces cooked shrimp or crabmeat, chopped
¼   green pepper, finely chopped
1   stalk celery, finely chopped
2   green onions, finely chopped
1   cup mayonnaise
¾   cup shredded Cheddar cheese
6   strips bacon, cooked and crumbled
6   sour dough English muffins, split

In a large bowl combine shrimp, green pepper, celery, onions, mayonnaise, cheese and bacon. Mix well. Place split muffins on a cookie sheet and divide shrimp mixture equally on the top of the muffins. Broil 3 minutes. Be careful not to let them burn.

Serves 6

MOROCCAN SANDWICH

No need to slight nutrition when you are in a hurry. The ingredients for this sandwich are quick-and-easy to put together.

2   tablespoons butter
¼   cup sliced almonds
1   pound ground beef
1   small onion, chopped
½   cup tomato paste
½   cup chili sauce
½   cup water
¼   cup raisins
¼   teaspoon cinnamon
½   teaspoon cumin
    salt
    pepper
    pita bread

In a large skillet melt butter and stir-fry almonds until golden. Remove almonds with a slotted spoon and set aside. In the same skillet sauté meat and onions until brown. Add tomato paste, chili sauce, water, raisins, cinnamon, cumin, salt and pepper. Cook this mixture for 5 minutes and then add almonds. To serve, cut the pita bread in halves and fill the pockets with the meat mixture. Garnish with lettuce, tomato and cheese.

Serves 6

GARNISHES

shredded lettuce
diced tomato
Monterey Jack cheese, shredded

FRENCH TOASTED CHICKEN SANDWICHES

You may wish to substitute turkey or water packed white tuna for the chicken.

1   cup chopped cooked chicken
½   cup minced celery
¼   cup chopped sweet pickle
1   teaspoon salt
    dash of pepper
¼   cup mayonnaise
12 slices white bread
3   eggs, beaten
½   cup milk
1   teaspoon sugar
¼   teaspoon salt
    butter or margarine

In a bowl combine chicken, celery, pickle, salt, pepper and mayonnaise. Mix well. Make 6 sandwiches using chicken mixture and bread. In a shallow dish whisk eggs, milk, sugar and salt together. Dip each sandwich into the egg mixture being sure to coat each side completely. In a large skillet, fry sandwiches in butter on both sides until filling is heated through and sandwiches are a golden brown (340° for an electric fry pan).

Serves 6

Entrées

PEPPER STEAK

1½ pounds flank or round steak, cut into ½-inch wide strips
2 tablespoons oil
1 tablespoon flour
¼ cup ketchup
¾ cup water
3 tablespoons soy sauce
1 beef bouillon cube
⅛ teaspoon pepper
1 onion, sliced and separated into rings
1 green pepper, sliced into rings
1 cup fresh mushrooms, sliced

In a large skillet brown the meat in oil over medium-high heat. Remove the meat and drain off excess grease from skillet. Add flour, ketchup, water, soy sauce, bouillon cube and pepper to the skillet. Stir constantly until mixture boils. Return the meat to the skillet and add the onions. Cover and simmer 30 minutes or until meat is tender. Add green peppers and simmer an additional 5 to 10 minutes. Pepper rings should be tender, but crisp. Five minutes before serving, stir in the mushrooms. Cook until barely soft. Serve over steamed rice.

Serves 4 to 6

BROILED FLANK STEAK

In the Southwest, outdoor cooking is a favorite and delicious way to prepare a meal because it keeps the heat out of the kitchen! Try this recipe for your next barbecue.

1 2-3 pound flank steak
¼ cup soy sauce
3 tablespoons honey
2 tablespoons vinegar
½ teaspoon garlic salt
1½ teaspoons ground ginger
½ cup vegetable oil
1 onion, finely chopped
½ cup beer

Score meat and place in a large shallow casserole. Combine remaining ingredients in blender or food processor. Blend well and pour over meat. Cover and marinate meat at least 6 hours, preferably overnight. During the marinating process turn the meat several times. Grill over hot coals or broil 6 to 7 minutes on each side. Slice on the diagonal to serve.

Serves 6 to 8

SICILIANO LIVER AND ONIONS

1   pound calves liver, thinly
      sliced
½   cup dry white wine
¼   teaspoon oregano
6   tablespoons olive oil
4   medium onions, sliced
½   cup plus 1 tablespoon flour
      salt
      pepper

Marinate liver in wine and oregano for approximately 1 hour in the refrigerator. In a large skillet heat 4 tablespoons oil and sauté onions until brown. Remove onions and set aside. Add 2 more tablespoons oil to the skillet. Drain liver reserving marinade. Dredge liver in ½ cup flour that has been seasoned with salt and pepper. Shake to remove excess flour and sauté in hot oil about 2 to 4 minutes on each side. *Do not overcook.* Add more oil if necessary. Remove to a warm platter and cover with reserved onions. Add the remaining 1 tablespoon of flour and the reserved marinade to the skillet. Cook, stirring occasionally, until thickened. Pour the sauce over the liver and onions.

Serves 4 to 6

NEVADA-STYLE SHORT RIBS

You may brown the meat, add marinade and refrigerate overnight before cooking.

3   pounds beef short ribs (or
      pork ribs)
1   onion, minced
¼   cup tarragon wine vinegar
2   tablespoons brown sugar
1   cup ketchup
½   cup water
3   tablespoons Worcestershire
      sauce
1   teaspoon prepared mustard
2   teaspoons salt

Using a heavy skillet, brown ribs slowly turning frequently and draining off excess fat as it accumulates. Place browned ribs in a shallow casserole. In a small bowl combine remaining ingredients and pour over the ribs. Cover and bake in a preheated 325° oven for 1½ to 2 hours or until meat is tender. Baste occasionally.

Serves 4

CARBONNADES À LA FLAMANDE

Cold winter nights call for warm fare. This entrée not only warms but satisfies both the heartiest and the most discriminating appetites.

4   pounds beef round steak or boneless rump roast, cut into ½-inch slices
½   cup flour
½   cup vegetable oil
2   large onions, sliced in ½-inch slices
6   garlic cloves, crushed
4   tablespoons red wine vinegar
3   tablespoons brown sugar
½   cup minced parsley
2   bay leaves
2   teaspoons thyme
1   tablespoon salt
1½ teaspoons pepper
2½ cups beef broth
3   cups dark beer

Dredge beef slices in flour. In a large skillet heat oil over medium-high heat and brown beef quickly. Transfer meat to a deep ovenproof casserole. Remove and discard all but 1 tablespoon of the grease from the skillet. Lightly brown onions in skillet and add to casserole. In the same skillet lightly brown garlic. Add 2 tablespoons of the vinegar and all of the sugar, herbs, seasonings and broth. Bring to a boil, stirring constantly. Add contents of skillet and the beer to the casserole. Bake covered in a preheated 325° oven for 2 hours. Remove casserole from oven and transfer to stove top. Stir in remaining 2 tablespoons vinegar and over medium heat bring sauce to a boil.

DUMPLINGS

2   cups self-rising flour, sifted
1¼ cups milk
2   tablespoons melted butter

While casserole is coming to a boil, combine all dumpling ingredients in a bowl and mix well. Drop dumpling batter by tablespoonfuls on top of the stew. Cover, reduce heat and cook for 15 minutes. Do not remove cover during this cooking process. Serve directly from casserole.

Serves 8

SIRLOIN BORDELAISE

This is a simple yet elegant house specialty of the contributor.

1   2 to 2½ pound sirloin steak,
    1¼-inches thick, cut into 4 to
    6 serving pieces
1   tablespoon vegetable oil
8   tablespoons butter
1   tablespoon finely chopped
    green onion
⅔   cup red wine
    minced parsley

Over medium-high heat combine oil and 2 tablespoons butter in a large skillet. When foam subsides, add steaks and sauté 4 to 5 minutes per side for medium rare. Remove steaks to a heated platter and keep warm. Pour grease out of skillet. Add 2 more tablespoons of butter to the pan and sauté the chopped onions over low heat for 1 to 2 minutes, until they are tender but not brown. Add wine and boil over high heat until the mixture is the consistency of a syrup and reduced in volume to about ⅓ cup. Remove the pan from the heat. Using a wire whisk beat in 4 tablespoons of butter, *one tablespoon at a time.* Each tablespoon of butter should be completely incorporated into the sauce before adding another tablespoon. Add any accumulated juices from steaks to sauce. Pour sauce over the steaks and garnish with chopped parsley.

Serves 4 to 6

VENISON JERKY

This is a very hot and spicy jerky.

½ cup soy sauce
4 tablespoons lemon pepper
1 teaspoon cayenne pepper
1 teaspoon crushed red pepper
2 garlic cloves, minced
¼ teaspoon Tabasco
¼ teaspoon pepper
¼ cup water
  dash of liquid smoke
  flavoring
2 pounds venison, thinly sliced
  with the grain

Combine all ingredients except meat and mix well. Add meat and marinate for 2 hours. Cover the bottom of the oven with foil and preheat to 150°. Lay marinated meat strips directly on oven racks and bake for 8 hours or until dry. Store in jars.

Makes 2 quart jars

SAUTÉED VENISON

Nevada enjoys both the terrain and climate to support a wide variety of wildlife including mule deer. If you are fortunate enough to have venison on hand, you will enjoy this easy-to-prepare dish.

9 tablespoons cider vinegar
  water
4-6 venison steaks or chops
2 cups flour (seasoned with
  onion salt, garlic salt, salt
  and pepper)
3 tablespoons vegetable oil
4 tablespoons red wine
4 tablespoons hot water

In a large shallow baking dish combine 3 tablespoons of the vinegar with enough water to cover venison. Soak the venison for 3 to 6 hours to remove gamey flavor. Change the water and vinegar mixture 2 more times during the soaking period using the same proportions of vinegar and water. Remove meat from the liquid and pat dry. Dredge venison in seasoned flour. In a large skillet heat the oil and fry venison, turning once, until crispy and brown on both sides. Add wine and water. Cover and simmer on low heat for about 1 hour.

Serves 4

FRUITED LAMB CHOPS

For good flavor and dollar-wise value, try these lamb chops cut from the shoulder. They are delicious and have a moist tenderness.

6 shoulder lamb chops, ½ to
   ¾-inch thick
¼ cup flour
2 tablespoons vegetable oil
1 teaspoon salt
½ teaspoon thyme
¼ teaspoon marjoram
¼ teaspoon pepper
½ cup brown sugar, firmly
   packed
1 tablespoon cornstarch
1 teaspoon pumpkin pie spice
1 cup water
3 tablespoons lemon juice
1 8-ounce package mixed dried
   fruit

Dredge lamb chops in flour. In a large skillet heat oil and brown chops. Place chops in a 2-quart ovenproof baking dish and sprinkle with salt, thyme, marjoram and pepper. Cover and bake in a preheated 350° oven for 30 minutes. In a small saucepan combine brown sugar, cornstarch and pumpkin pie spice. Add water and lemon juice. Cook, stirring constantly until sauce thickens. Boil for 3 minutes and stir in the dried fruit. Remove the lamb chops from the oven and skim off excess fat. Pour the fruit sauce over the lamb chops. Cover and bake for an additional 30 minutes.

Serves 6

RABBIT WITH MUSTARD

1 rabbit, cut in serving pieces
   salt
   pepper
4 tablespoons butter, softened
½ cup Dijon-style mustard
2 carrots, peeled and sliced
1 large onion, sliced
2 stalks celery, sliced
   several parsley sprigs
1 tablespoon thyme
½ bay leaf
⅛ teaspoon rosemary
½ cup dry white wine
⅔ cup heavy cream

Season the rabbit with salt and pepper. Rub with butter and place in a shallow roasting pan. Roast in a preheated 425° oven for 20 minutes, basting with pan juices. Remove from the oven and generously coat with mustard. Surround the rabbit with the sliced vegetables, parsley, thyme, bay leaf and rosemary. Return the meat to the oven and immediately reduce oven temperature to 350°. Roast another 40 minutes basting occasionally with the pan juices. Transfer the rabbit and vegetables to a serving platter. Stir the wine into the pan juices and boil 2 minutes, then stir in the cream. Heat, but do not boil. Salt and pepper to taste. Strain the sauce and serve with the rabbit.

Serves 4 to 6

LEG OF LAMB WITH SPINACH AND APRICOTS

Delight the most discriminating of guests with this savory, show-off entrée.

½ pound dried apricots
3 pounds spinach, washed and trimmed of stems
1 medium onion, chopped
2 cups fresh bread crumbs
2 eggs, slightly beaten
½ cup butter or margarine, cut into cubes and softened
1 tablespoon grated lemon rind
1 tablespoon salt
⅛ teaspoon mace
  pepper
1 6-pound leg of lamb, boned but not butterflied
  vegetable oil
6 garlic cloves, peeled and slivered
½ cup beef broth

Soak apricots in a bowl of cold water for 4 hours. Drain and chop. In a large pot of boiling salted water blanch the spinach for 2 minutes. Drain and refresh under cold water. Squeeze excess water from spinach. Chop the spinach and combine with onions and apricots. Grind this mixture coarsely in a food processor. Place in a bowl and add bread crumbs, eggs, butter, lemon rind, salt, mace and pepper. Mix well. Sew closed the large opening in the boned leg of lamb. Through the small opening stuff the leg loosely with about 1½ cups of the apricot-spinach mixture. Put remaining stuffing in a buttered baking dish and cover with foil. Sew up the small opening and brush the lamb with oil. Place slivers of garlic randomly under the skin of the lamb. Place lamb in an oiled roasting pan and bake in a preheated 450° oven 30 to 45 minutes or until the internal meat temperature reaches 140° for medium rare. Bake the remaining stuffing with the roast. Transfer lamb to a cutting board, cover and let rest for 15 minutes before slicing. Skim fat from the roasting pan and add beef broth to pan drippings. Season with salt and pepper to taste. Cut lamb into ½-inch slices and spoon sauce over each slice.

Serves 6 to 8

ITALIAN SAUSAGE AND EGGPLANT

½ pound hot Italian sausage, casing removed
½ pound sweet Italian sausage, casing removed
½ cup olive oil
4 garlic cloves, minced
1 medium onion, finely chopped
1 6-ounce can tomato paste
2 16-ounce cans tomatoes, puréed
1 teaspoon salt
1 teaspoon coarsely ground pepper
1 teaspoon sugar
2 chicken bouillon cubes
½ teaspoon crushed basil
¼ teaspoon thyme
¼ teaspoon oregano
1 eggplant, peeled and diced
½ pound fresh mushrooms, sliced
½ green pepper, sliced
1 pound vermicelli

Cut sausages into bite-size pieces. In a skillet fry sausages until crisp. Drain and set aside. In a Dutch oven or large skillet heat olive oil and sauté garlic and onions lightly. Add tomato paste and continue cooking over low heat for 5 minutes stirring constantly. Add puréed tomatoes, salt, pepper, sugar, bouillon, basil, thyme and oregano to sauce. Stir well and simmer covered for 1 hour. Add sausage, eggplant, mushrooms and green pepper. Simmer covered for another hour. Cook vermicelli al dente. Serve sauce over hot pasta.

Serves 6 to 8

Planning ahead? Double your favorite casserole recipe. Freeze the extra casserole in its serving dish lined with foil. Once frozen, the contents can be easily removed, wrapped tightly and stored for use at a later date. The dish can now be used again and again until serving day.

PORK ROAST WITH MUSTARD SAUCE AND HONEY APPLES

The honey apples are a delicious accompaniment to this new version of the traditional pork roast.

½ cup Dijon-style mustard
2 tablespoons soy sauce
2 garlic cloves, minced
1 tablespoon sage
¼ teaspoon marjoram
1 5 pound pork roast, boned and tied

Combine the mustard, soy sauce, garlic, sage and marjoram. Mix well. Place pork in a roasting pan and spread with mustard mixture. Roast in a preheated 350° oven. After roasting for one hour begin to baste meat frequently with pan juices. Roast 30 to 35 minutes per pound or until a meat thermometer reads 170°.

HONEY APPLES

½ cup honey
2 tablespoons cider vinegar
¼ teaspoon salt
¼ teaspoon cinnamon
4 apples, peeled, cored and sliced ½-inch thick

Combine honey, vinegar, salt and cinnamon in a saucepan. Bring to a boil and add apples. Simmer 10 minutes and serve with the roast.

Serves 8

APPLE STUFFED PORK CHOPS

1 small apple, peeled, cored and diced
1 small onion, chopped
1 teaspoon salt
2 cups fresh bread crumbs
¼ teaspoon pepper
¼ teaspoon sage
3 tablespoons melted butter
6 thick pork chops
3 tablespoons vegetable oil

Combine apple, onion, salt, bread crumbs, pepper, sage and butter. If the mixture appears too dry to hold together, add a little water. Cut a deep pocket into the side of each pork chop and stuff with the apple dressing. Secure with a toothpick. In a large skillet brown the stuffed chops on each side in the vegetable oil. Place the chops in a shallow ovenproof casserole and arrange the remaining dressing around the chops. Bake in a preheated 350° oven for 1 hour.

Serves 4 to 6

SOUTHWEST SPARERIBS

Make this the main attraction for your summer cookout. Our testers raved about them.

3 pounds country-style spareribs
3 tablespoons olive oil
⅓ cup soy sauce
1 teaspoon ground ginger
½ cup whiskey
¼ cup pineapple juice
¼ cup packed brown sugar

In a large Dutch oven parboil the ribs for 20 minutes in water to cover. Combine the olive oil, soy sauce, ginger, whiskey, pineapple juice and brown sugar to make a marinade. Place ribs in a shallow dish and pour marinade mixture over them. Marinate meat overnight turning occasionally.

BARBECUE SAUCE

1 cup ketchup
¼ cup brown sugar
¼ cup Worcestershire sauce
¼ cup vinegar
1 tablespoon celery seed
1 teaspoon chili powder
   dash of pepper

Thoroughly combine the ketchup, brown sugar, Worcestershire sauce, vinegar, celery seed, chili powder and pepper. (If a thinner sauce is desired you may add a slight amount of water.) Remove meat from marinade and grill turning frequently to prevent burning. When almost cooked, baste several times with barbecue sauce on both sides. Warm any remaining sauce and serve with ribs.

Serves 4 to 6

GRILLED LEMON CHICKEN

Liberate yourself from last-minute preparations. Assemble this marinade early in the day and simply reheat it in a microwave oven just before basting the chicken.

¾ cup butter
½ cup lemon juice
⅓ cup water
1 teaspoon paprika
⅛ teaspoon cayenne pepper
2 tablespoons soy sauce
1 teaspoon honey
1 teaspoon Dijon-style mustard
2 garlic cloves, minced
½ teaspoon salt
2 whole frying chickens, quartered

In a small saucepan combine all ingredients except the chicken. Heat until butter melts. Mix well. Place chicken on a greased grill 5 to 6 inches from coals. Brush with marinade and grill 25 to 30 minutes or until chicken is done. Turn and baste frequently.

Serves 8

SWISS TARRAGON CHICKEN

Chicken is one of the family favorites busy cooks rely on. A few extra touches can transform a stand-by into a memorable meal. We present Swiss Tarragon Chicken . . .

4	tablespoons butter or margarine
1	tablespoon vegetable oil
4	chicken breast halves, skinned and boned
⅔	cup chicken broth
⅔	cup dry white wine
1½	teaspoons tarragon
½	pound mushrooms, sliced
4	thick slices home-style white bread
4	slices Swiss cheese
1½	teaspoons cornstarch
1	teaspoon water

Melt 2 tablespoons of the butter and the oil in a large skillet. Brown chicken pieces. Add broth, wine and tarragon and simmer covered for 20 to 30 minutes. While chicken is cooking, in a separate skillet, sauté the mushrooms in the remaining 2 tablespoons butter. Set aside. Place bread slices on a cookie sheet and bake in a preheated 250° oven until dry but not brown. When chicken is done, remove from skillet and place each piece on a slice of bread. Top with the Swiss cheese. Bake in a preheated 450° oven until cheese melts. In a small bowl mix cornstarch with water and add to sauce remaining in skillet. Cook over medium heat, stirring constantly, until sauce thickens. Add sautéed mushrooms to sauce and pour over chicken just before serving.

Serves 4

ABOVE THE LIGHTS

Artichoke Bottoms Gratinée

Oysters Rockefeller

Caesar's Salad

Breast of Chicken Siciliano

Orzo with Pesto

Banana Fritters

Petite Sirah

Entertaining takes on a special glow in this dining room, high on Sunrise Mountain overlooking the Las Vegas Valley.

Tableware courtesy of Bullock's Department Store

LEMON CHICKEN

2   lemons
4   chicken breast halves, skinned and boned
¼   cup flour
½   teaspoon paprika
2   tablespoons vegetable oil
2   tablespoons brown sugar
1½   teaspoons salt
½   cup chicken broth

Grate the rind from one lemon. Set aside. Cut the same lemon in half and squeeze the juice over the chicken breasts. Combine flour and paprika and dredge chicken in this mixture. In a large skillet heat oil and brown chicken on both sides. Sprinkle chicken with lemon rind, brown sugar and salt. Add broth to the skillet and bring to a simmer. Reduce heat to low, cover, and cook for 25 minutes. Slice remaining lemon and arrange over the chicken. Cover and continue to cook until chicken is fork tender and no longer pink.

Serves 2 to 4

SPICED CHICKEN

1   cup orange juice
1½   cups sliced peaches
2   tablespoons brown sugar
2   tablespoons vinegar
1   teaspoon nutmeg
1   teaspoon basil
1   garlic clove, minced
½   cup flour
1   teaspoon salt
⅛   teaspoon pepper
6   chicken legs
6   chicken thighs
¼   cup vegetable oil

Combine orange juice, peaches, brown sugar, vinegar, nutmeg, basil and garlic in a saucepan. Cook over low heat for 10 minutes. In a small bowl mix together the flour, salt and pepper. Dredge the chicken pieces in this mixture. In a large skillet heat oil and brown chicken on all sides. Drain off excess oil and cover chicken with the warmed fruit sauce. Cover skillet and simmer for 20 to 30 minutes or until done.

Serves 4 to 6

PARMESAN CHICKEN

6 chicken breast halves, skinned and boned
6 slices Monterey Jack cheese, ¼-inch thick
½ cup plus 2 tablespoons butter or margarine
2 tablespoons Dijon-style mustard
1 cup dry bread crumbs
1 cup freshly grated Parmesan cheese
¼ cup minced parsley
½ cup flour
  salt
  pepper

Cut a pocket in each chicken breast and insert a piece of Monterey Jack cheese. In a small saucepan melt ½ cup butter. Stir in mustard. In a separate bowl combine bread crumbs, Parmesan cheese and parsley. Dust chicken with flour and dip in melted butter. Roll in the bread crumb mixture. In a large skillet melt the remaining 2 tablespoons of butter and brown chicken lightly on all sides. Place chicken in an ovenproof casserole. Salt and pepper to taste. Bake in a preheated 350° oven for 30 minutes.

Serves 6

CHICKEN AND LINGUINE

½ cup butter or margarine
2 garlic cloves, minced
1 tablespoon basil
12 chicken thighs
2 10-ounce packages frozen chopped spinach, cooked and drained
1 pound linguine, cooked, drained and kept warm
1 cup freshly grated Parmesan cheese
  salt
  pepper
1 orange, quartered

In a preheated 400° oven melt butter in a 9 × 13-inch dish. Remove from oven and stir garlic and basil into melted butter. Place chicken in dish skin side up. Bake uncovered for 45 minutes or until chicken is well browned. Baste several times during baking with pan drippings. When chicken is done, remove from dish and keep warm. Add spinach to drippings stirring well. Add the cooked linguine and Parmesan cheese to spinach. Mix well and season with salt and pepper. To serve, mound linguine on individual plates and accompany with 3 chicken thighs and an orange wedge. Just before eating, squeeze the orange over the chicken and linguine.

Serves 4

CHICKEN KIEV

1   tablespoon minced parsley
½   tablespoon chopped chives
½   teaspoon tarragon
1   garlic clove, mashed
½   cup butter, softened
6   chicken breast halves,
     skinned and boned
1   egg
1   tablespoon water
1   tablespoon vegetable oil
½   cup flour
2   cups fresh bread crumbs
     oil for deep frying

Combine parsley, chives, tarragon, garlic and butter. Shape into a 2 × 3-inch rectangle and chill for 30 minutes or until firm. Place chicken breasts between waxed paper and pound thin (about ¼-inch). Cut butter mixture into 6 pieces. Place 1 piece in the center of each chicken breast. Fold lower edge of meat over butter, fold in sides and roll up to enclose filling. (Chicken pieces differ in size, so you may have to remove some of the butter filling in order to wrap meat securely.) Beat egg together with water and oil. Coat chicken with flour, then dip in egg mixture and roll in bread crumbs. Chill at least one hour. In a deep fat fryer, heat about 2 inches of oil to 360°. Fry chicken pieces two at a time for 5 minutes or until chicken is no longer pink. Drain chicken well and place on platter. Keep warm while preparing remaining pieces.

Serves 4 to 6

To give your barbecued chicken or lamb a special flavor, use sprigs of rosemary as a basting brush. Then, just before the meat is done, drop sprigs into the hot coals and watch the appetites flare!

BAKED CHICKEN CURRY

Because this dish is so distinctive in flavor, it needs only steamed rice and a fresh fruit salad to complete the menu.

3 tablespoons butter or margarine, melted
3 tablespoons milk
¼ cup prepared mustard
½ cup honey
2 teaspoons curry powder
1 teaspoon salt
  dash white pepper
1 whole frying chicken, cut in serving pieces
½ cup raisins
¼ cup chopped nuts
¼ cup shredded coconut

Combine butter, milk, mustard, honey, curry, salt and pepper. Coat chicken pieces with this mixture and place in a well-greased ovenproof casserole. Bake in a preheated 350° oven for 1¼ hours. Baste with the pan drippings several times during the cooking process. During the last 15 minutes of baking, sprinkle raisins, chopped nuts and coconut on top.

Serves 4

CHICKEN ALL'ITALIANA

After assembling this dish, it may be refrigerated up to two days before final cooking. We like serving it with a pasta sprinkled with freshly grated Parmesan cheese.

2½ pounds chicken pieces
1 teaspoon salt
¼ teaspoon pepper
1 tablespoon vegetable oil
1 pound sweet Italian sausage, cut in bite-size pieces
2 16-ounce cans Italian plum tomatoes, drained
½ cup chicken broth
1 cup chopped onion
1 green pepper, cut in 1-inch squares
1 teaspoon minced garlic
1 teaspoon oregano
1 teaspoon basil
1 teaspoon sugar

Sprinkle chicken with salt and pepper. In a large skillet heat oil and brown chicken. Remove chicken and set aside. Brown sausage and drain. Pour off grease from skillet and add all remaining ingredients. Mix well. Arrange browned chicken and sausage over contents in skillet. Cover and simmer 30 to 40 minutes or until chicken is done.

Serves 6

CHICKEN ALMOND VERMICELLI

1   tablespoon butter or
    margarine
2   whole chicken breasts,
    skinned, boned and cut into
    ¼-inch strips
1½ cups sliced fresh mushrooms
1   cup diagonally sliced celery
1   large onion, cut into 8
    wedges
½   cup sliced water chestnuts
1¼ cups chicken broth
2½ cups diagonally sliced
    broccoli spears
2   tablespoons cornstarch
2   tablespoons soy sauce
¾   teaspoon salt
½   pound vermicelli, cooked,
    drained and kept warm
2   tablespoons slivered almonds,
    toasted

Using a wok or electric skillet melt butter over
high heat. Stirring constantly, sauté chicken 3 to 4
minutes or until meat is no longer pink. Remove
chicken with a slotted spoon to a warm platter.
Add mushrooms to wok and cook until slightly
softened. Add celery, onion and water chestnuts.
Cook 2 to 3 minutes. Stir in broth, broccoli and
sautéed chicken. In a small bowl whisk together
cornstarch, soy sauce and salt. Add to wok and stir
well. Bring to a boil and cook mixture until liquid
is clear and slightly thickened. To serve, arrange
vermicelli on a warmed platter and top with
chicken mixture. Garnish with toasted slivered
almonds.

Serves 6

CRAB AND WILD RICE CASSEROLE

½   pound cooked crab meat
1   cup cooked wild rice
½   cup mayonnaise
2   eggs, beaten
½   cup milk or half and half
¼   cup minced onion
¼   cup minced celery
½   cup sliced stuffed olives
    salt
    pepper
½   teaspoon ginger
½   cup dry bread crumbs
1   tablespoon butter, melted

Into a large bowl flake crab meat and mix with
rice and mayonnaise. Combine eggs and milk and
add to crab mixture. Stir in onion, celery, olives,
salt, pepper and ginger. Pour into a greased 1-
quart casserole. Combine bread crumbs and melted
butter and sprinkle over all. Bake in a preheated
350° oven for 30 minutes.

Serves 2 to 4

COQUILLE ST. JACQUES

1½ cups shredded Gruyère cheese
1 cup mayonnaise
¼ cup dry white wine
1 tablespoon minced parsley
4 tablespoons butter or margarine
1 pound sea scallops, quartered
½ pound mushrooms, sliced
½ cup chopped onion
½ cup fresh bread crumbs
1 tablespoon melted butter

Combine cheese, mayonnaise, white wine and minced parsley. Mix well and set aside. In a large skillet heat 2 tablespoons butter. Sauté scallops just until opaque. Remove from skillet and drain. Heat 2 more tablespoons of butter in the skillet. Sauté mushrooms and onion for 3 minutes. Add to cheese mixture. Arrange scallops in an ovenproof casserole or individual scallop shells. Cover with cheese and mushroom mixture. Toss bread crumbs with the melted butter and sprinkle over casserole. Broil 6 inches from heat for 2 to 3 minutes or until lightly browned and bubbly.

Serves 4 to 6

SCALLOPS AND MUSHROOMS

If serving a crowd, you will have no difficulty in doubling this recipe. Either bay or sea scallops may be used depending upon the season.

2½ pounds scallops
    water
1¼ pounds fresh mushrooms, sliced
5 tablespoons butter
2½ tablespoons flour
1¾ cups heavy cream
½ teaspoon salt
¼ teaspoon pepper
¾ teaspoon Worcestershire sauce

Rinse scallops and cut in half if large. In a 3-quart saucepan cover scallops with cold water and heat slowly to the boiling point. Remove from heat, drain immediately and set aside. In a large skillet melt butter and sauté mushrooms for 5 minutes or until browned. Add flour and cook 5 minutes stirring constantly. Gradually add cream and continue to stir until sauce thickens. Stir in scallops, salt, pepper and Worcestershire sauce. Serve on toast points for brunch or over rice for a dinner entrée.

Serves 6 to 8

MAMA MIA'S FETTUCCINE

Complete your menu with a tangy salad and crusty rolls.

6   large garlic cloves, minced

4   tablespoons butter

½   cup olive oil

1   cup diced cooked ham or prosciutto

1   cup heavy cream

4   tablespoons freshly grated Parmesan cheese

4   tablespoons grated Romano cheese

½   teaspoon salt

1   teaspoon coarsely ground pepper

½   pound sliced mushrooms (optional)

1   pound spinach fettuccine, cooked, drained and kept warm

    Parmesan cheese

    crushed red pepper (optional)

Sauté garlic in butter and oil until soft, but not brown. Add ham, cream, grated cheeses, salt, pepper and mushrooms. Stir well and simmer briefly to blend flavors. Place the pasta in a large bowl and pour sauce over all. Toss together and sprinkle with Parmesan cheese and crushed red pepper.

Serves 6

Fresh garlic can be minced in quantity for future use. In a food processor, mince the peeled cloves from 2 to 3 garlic bulbs. Put in a jar, drizzle a very thin layer of olive oil over the garlic, cover and refrigerate.

THIN CRUST HOMEMADE PIZZA

The dough for our Thin Crust Homemade Pizza may also be used for breadsticks. Depending on the desired length, pinch off pieces of dough and roll into breadstick shapes. Brush each piece with olive oil and roll in seasoned salt. Bake at 425° for 8 minutes or until crisp and brown.

CRUST

2   packages active dry yeast
    pinch of sugar
1¼ cups lukewarm water (110°-115°)
3½ cups unbleached flour
1½ teaspoons salt
¼   cup plus 1 tablespoon olive oil

Stir yeast and sugar into ¼ cup lukewarm water. Set in a warm place until yeast bubbles and doubles in volume, about 10 minutes. Stir together flour and salt in a large mixing bowl. Make a well in the center of the dry ingredients and pour in yeast mixture, 1 cup lukewarm water and ¼ cup of the olive oil. Mix until a rough ball forms. Turn dough out onto a floured surface and knead for about 10 minutes or until dough is elastic and shiny. Grease the inside of a ceramic bowl with the remaining 1 tablespoon olive oil. Place dough in bowl turning once to oil all sides. Cover with a cloth and let rise in a warm place for 1 to 1½ hours or until dough has doubled in bulk.

SAUCE

2   16-ounce cans Italian plum tomatoes
3   tablespoons olive oil
1   cup minced onion
3   garlic cloves, minced
1   6-ounce can tomato paste
1   tablespoon oregano
1   tablespoon basil
1   large bay leaf
2   teaspoons sugar
1   tablespoon salt
¼   teaspoon pepper

Drain and chop tomatoes reserving juice. Heat oil in heavy saucepan. Add onion and cook over medium heat until soft. Add chopped tomatoes, garlic, tomato paste, oregano, basil, bay leaf, sugar, salt, pepper and reserved tomato juice. Simmer uncovered for 1 hour.

(continued on next page)

ASSEMBLY AND TOPPING

  flour
3 tablespoons cornmeal
3 cups shredded mozzarella
  cheese
  sliced green pepper
  sliced mushrooms
  sliced onions
  Italian sausage, browned and
  crumbled
3 tablespoons freshly grated
  Parmesan cheese
3 teaspoons olive oil

Punch down pizza dough and divide into 3 equal portions. Working with one piece at a time, knead briefly on a lightly floured board. Pick up and stretch dough in a circular motion. Return to board and flatten into a rectangular shape. Roll out into a 9 × 12-inch rectangle. Sprinkle 1 teaspoon cornmeal on a cookie sheet and place dough on it crimping edges. Spread ⅓ of the pizza sauce over dough. Cover with 1 cup mozzarella cheese and other toppings as desired. Finally, sprinkle with 1 tablespoon Parmesan cheese and 1 teaspoon olive oil. Bake in a preheated 500° oven 10 to 12 minutes. Repeat the process for the remaining 2 pieces of dough.

Makes 3

SPAGHETTI ALL'AMATRICIANA

If pancetta is available in your area, substitute it for the bacon. This will make for an even more authentic Italian flavor.

4 tablespoons olive oil
1 onion, finely chopped
1 red pepper, cut in strips
1 garlic clove, minced
2 tablespoons minced parsley
½ pound bacon, cut into ¼-
  inch strips
1 pound fresh tomatoes, peeled
  and chopped (1 16-ounce can
  Italian plum tomatoes can be
  substituted)
  freshly ground pepper
  salt
12 ounces spaghetti
4 tablespoons freshly grated
  Parmesan cheese

In a large saucepan heat 2 tablespoons olive oil. Add onion, red pepper, garlic, parsley and bacon. Sauté for 5 minutes stirring often. Add tomatoes and pepper. Simmer uncovered for 15 minutes. Add salt to taste. Cook spaghetti al dente. Drain and place in a hot bowl. Sprinkle the remaining 2 tablespoons olive oil and the Parmesan cheese over the spaghetti and toss. Place on a large serving platter or individual plates. Spoon sauce over spaghetti and serve.

Serves 4

HOT PEPPER CHICKEN WITH CHINESE PANCAKES

1 whole chicken breast, skinned and boned
1 tablespoon cornstarch
1 tablespoon soy sauce
1 egg white
2 garlic cloves, mashed

Cut chicken in ½-inch strips. Set aside. In a large bowl combine cornstarch, soy sauce, egg white and garlic. Add chicken and toss well. Cover and chill.

SEASONING SAUCE

1 teaspoon cornstarch
¼ teaspoon ground ginger
1 tablespoon dry Sherry
2 tablespoons soy sauce
2 tablespoons sugar
2 teaspoons red wine vinegar

Whisk together cornstarch, ginger, Sherry, soy sauce, sugar and vinegar. Set aside.

CHINESE PANCAKES

1½ cups flour
½ cup lukewarm water (110°-115°)
 vegetable shortening
½ cup minced green onions
2 tablespoons vegetable oil

In a large bowl mix flour with water. Turn dough out on a floured surface and knead 5 minutes or until dough is smooth and elastic. Divide into 8 equal portions. Roll each piece into a very thin sheet. Lightly brush sheets with vegetable shortening and sprinkle with onions. Roll dough up jelly-roll style and tuck ends under to meet. Again roll out the dough, but this time into a 5-inch round thin pancake. In a small skillet over medium heat add oil. When oil is hot, brown pancakes about 1½ to 2 minutes on each side. Add more oil to skillet as necessary.

(continued on next page)

PREPARATION

2-4 small dried hot chile peppers
4 tablespoons peanut oil
 chilled marinated chicken
1 large green pepper, seeded and sliced in ¼-inch strips
 seasoning sauce
½ cup unsalted whole cashews
 Hoisin sauce
8 Chinese pancakes
 chopped green onions

Slit chile peppers lengthwise and remove seeds. Heat oil in wok and cook hot peppers until black. Discard peppers. Add more oil to wok if necessary and stir-fry chicken 2 minutes. Add green pepper and stir-fry 2 minutes. Add seasoning sauce and stir until mixture boils. Blend in nuts just before serving. To serve, spread a teaspoon of Hoisin sauce across each pancake. Top with the chicken and garnish with green onions. Fold the Chinese pancakes over the filling and enjoy.

Serves 4

KOREAN PORK AND SPINACH

Do your dicing and measuring early in the day, go play, and then put together this "honorable" blend of pork, vegetables and spices.

2 tablespoons peanut oil
2 pounds lean pork, diced
2 garlic cloves, minced
2 bunches spinach, rinsed, drained and trimmed of stems
¼ cup soy sauce
1 teaspoon freshly grated ginger root
 salt
 pepper
6 green onions, chopped
2 eggs, lightly beaten
2 teaspoons toasted sesame seeds
 steamed rice

Heat oil in wok. Add pork and garlic. Stir-fry until pork is seared. Add spinach, soy sauce, ginger, salt and pepper. Stir-fry for 1 minute. Cover and simmer briefly until spinach is tender. Remove cover and stir in green onions and egg. Stir-fry an additional 2 minutes. Sprinkle with toasted sesame seeds and serve with steamed rice.

Serves 6 to 8

MINCED CHICKEN

6   ounces chicken meat, minced
6   ounces pork loin, minced
3   chicken livers, minced
¼   teaspoon black pepper
1   egg yolk
½   cup chopped bamboo shoots
½   cup chopped water chestnuts
1   tablespoon chopped Chinese
    black mushrooms, softened
    in water
1   teaspoon salt
1   tablespoon soy sauce
½   teaspoon sugar
1   teaspoon sesame oil
1   teaspoon cornstarch
2   tablespoons water
4   tablespoons peanut oil
1   tablespoon chopped green
    onion
1   tablespoon chopped ginger
    root
1   tablespoon rice wine
    oil for deep frying
1   ounce rice noodles
24 lettuce leaves

In a large bowl combine meats with black pepper, egg yolk, bamboo shoots, water chestnuts and mushrooms. Mix well and set aside. In a small bowl whisk together the salt, soy sauce, sugar, sesame oil, cornstarch and water. In a wok or large skillet heat the 4 tablespoons of peanut oil. Stir-fry green onion and ginger until fragrant. Add meat mixture and stir-fry over high heat until dry. Add soy sauce mixture and rice wine. Stir-fry briefly and reduce heat to warm. In a deep fryer or skillet heat enough oil to fry noodles. Over medium heat fry noodles until golden brown on both sides. Remove from oil and drain well.

To serve, place fried noodles in center of a large platter. Arrange stir-fried meat and vegetables on top. To eat, wrap a portion of the meat, vegetables and noodles in a leaf of lettuce.

Serves 6

You will always have ginger root on hand if you simply seal tightly in plastic wrap and freeze. When called for in a recipe, remove ginger root from freezer, grate or slice off the amount needed, re-wrap and return to the freezer.

INDIA CURRY

Four cups of cooked chicken cut into bite-size pieces may be substituted for the shrimp and lemon juice.

½	cup chopped onion
5	tablespoons butter or margarine
6	tablespoons flour
4	teaspoons curry powder
1	teaspoon salt
1	teaspoon sugar
¼	teaspoon ground ginger
1	cup chicken broth
2	cups half and half
4	cups cooked whole small shrimp
1	teaspoon lemon juice
	cooked rice

In a large skillet over medium heat sauté onion in butter until tender. Blend in flour, curry, salt, sugar and ginger. Cook briefly. Add broth and half and half. Reduce heat to low and cook, stirring constantly, 5 to 10 minutes until mixture thickens. Add shrimp and lemon juice. Simmer over low heat until shrimp are heated through. Serve over rice and accompany with your choice of condiments.

Serves 6

CONDIMENTS

shredded coconut
chopped peanuts
hard-boiled egg yolks
bacon, cooked and crumbled
chopped chiles
bananas
chutney

ARTICHOKE BOTTOMS GRATINÉE

One of the charms of this accompaniment is that the artichokes and mushrooms may be sautéed and assembled in advance. Just before serving sprinkle with cheese and broil. For a quick to prepare but impressive dinner, serve them with our Sirloin Bordelaise.

1	14-ounce can artichoke bottoms, drained
2	tablespoons butter or margarine
½	cup finely chopped mushrooms
4	tablespoons grated Gruyère or Swiss cheese

In a skillet sauté artichoke bottoms in butter. With a slotted spoon remove artichokes from skillet and keep warm in an ovenproof dish. Add mushrooms to skillet and sauté for 5 minutes. Place an equal portion of the mushrooms on top of each artichoke bottom. Sprinkle with grated cheese and place under the broiler until cheese melts. Serve at once.

Serves 6 to 8

MARINATED ASPARAGUS

Spring is the time for asparagus in all its green succulence. We feature it with a tangy marinade.

1	pound asparagus
¾	cup olive oil
¼	cup white wine vinegar
1	tablespoon Dijon-style mustard
	salt
	pepper
3	shallots, finely chopped
2	tablespoons chopped capers
¼	cup minced parsley
2	tablespoons chopped fresh mint
1	teaspoon dill
½	teaspoon basil
½	teaspoon tarragon
½	teaspoon thyme
1	hard boiled egg, chopped

Snap tough ends off asparagus stems and discard. Cook asparagus in a small amount of water until tender but crisp. Cool. Combine all remaining ingredients in a food processor or blender. Process about 15 seconds. Arrange asparagus flat in a shallow serving dish. Pour marinade over all, cover and refrigerate several hours or overnight. When ready to serve, remove asparagus from marinade and place on a serving platter. Garnish with chopped egg and lace with a small amount of marinade.

Serves 4

CHILLED GREEN BEANS VINAIGRETTE

1½ pounds fresh green beans
1   tablespoon freshly grated
    onion
1¼ teaspoons salt
¾   teaspoon ground pepper
1   tablespoon Dijon-style
    mustard
2   tablespoons red wine vinegar
¾   cup olive oil
½   teaspoon fresh lemon juice

Snap green beans into 2-inch sections. Steam for 8 minutes. Drain and rinse with cold water. Refrigerate. In a bowl combine onion, salt, ground pepper, mustard and vinegar. Whisk in the oil one tablespoon at a time. Whisk in lemon juice. Pour dressing over beans, toss lightly and serve. Marinated beans may be refrigerated overnight if you wish.

Serves 6

BROCCOLI À LA DON

1   large bunch fresh broccoli,
    cut into bite-size pieces (2
    10-ounce packages frozen
    chopped broccoli may be
    substituted)
¼   teaspoon garlic powder
4   tablespoons butter or
    margarine
2   tablespoons flour
1   cup milk
1   cup grated Cheddar cheese
15 onion crackers, crushed
½   cup freshly grated Parmesan
    cheese

Cook broccoli until just tender. Drain, season with garlic powder and set aside. To prepare sauce, melt 2 tablespoons of the butter in a saucepan. Over low heat add 2 tablespoons flour and whisk until well blended. Add milk and whisk until smooth. Cook over medium heat until sauce thickens. Slowly add Cheddar cheese and stir sauce until cheese has melted. Remove from heat. Arrange half of the broccoli in the bottom of an ovenproof casserole. Sprinkle with half of the cracker crumbs and half of the Parmesan cheese. Dot with 1 tablespoon of the remaining butter. Repeat each layer. Pour sauce over all. Bake covered in a preheated 350° oven for 20 minutes.

Serves 6

BROCCOLI-CAULIFLOWER SUPREME

1 medium bunch broccoli, cut into bite-size pieces
1 medium head cauliflower, trimmed and separated into flowerets
½ pound bacon, cooked and crumbled
¼ cup slivered almonds
2 tablespoons butter or margarine
2 tablespoons flour
1 teaspoon salt
½ teaspoon white pepper
2 cups milk
¾ cup grated Cheddar cheese
2 cups buttered bread crumbs

Cook broccoli until tender. Drain and arrange in the bottom of a 9 x 13-inch ovenproof baking dish. Cook cauliflower until tender. Drain and place on top of the broccoli. Sprinkle bacon and almonds over the broccoli and cauliflower. To prepare cheese sauce melt butter in a saucepan. Add flour and whisk for 2 minutes over medium heat. Stir in salt and pepper. Add milk. Continue cooking over medium heat whisking sauce occasionally until it thickens and begins to bubble. Add cheese, stirring until melted. Pour the sauce over the vegetables and top with the buttered bread crumbs. Bake uncovered in a preheated 350° oven for 20 to 30 minutes or until heated through.

Serves 6 to 8

LEMON DRESSING FOR BROCCOLI

¼ cup lemon juice
¼ cup vegetable oil
¼ teaspoon paprika
1 teaspoon sugar
½ teaspoon salt
1 garlic clove, crushed
1 tablespoon finely chopped onion
cooked broccoli

In a food processor or blender combine all ingredients. Blend well and chill for at least 2 hours. Pour dressing over cooked broccoli. The broccoli may be served warm or chilled.

Makes ½ cup

DOUBLE ORANGE CARROTS

10 medium carrots, peeled and sliced on the diagonal
2 tablespoons sugar
2 teaspoons cornstarch
½ teaspoon salt
½ teaspoon ground ginger
½ cup orange juice
4 tablespoons butter or margarine

Cook carrots just until tender. Drain and keep warm. In a small saucepan combine sugar, cornstarch, salt, ginger and orange juice. Stir constantly over medium heat until thickened. Boil one minute and stir in butter. Pour over hot carrots and toss to coat thoroughly.

Serves 6

CAULIFLOWER ITALIANO

1 large head cauliflower, trimmed and separated into flowerets
2 cups dried seasoned bread crumbs
4 tablespoons freshly grated Parmesan cheese
1 teaspoon garlic salt
½ teaspoon pepper
1 egg
1 cup milk
¼ cup vegetable oil

Steam cauliflower until just tender. Drain and let cool. In a shallow dish combine bread crumbs, Parmesan cheese, garlic salt and pepper. Mix well. In a large bowl beat egg and milk together. Dip cooled flowerets in the egg-milk mixture and roll in the bread crumbs. In a large skillet heat oil over medium-high heat. Add all of the flowerets to the skillet, frying until golden brown on one side. They will adhere to one another. To cook the other side, invert the skillet on to a platter. Return pan to heat and slide uncooked side of flowerets back into the skillet. Fry until golden. To serve, slip cooked cauliflower onto a round platter.

Serves 4

DEEP FRIED CAULIFLOWER WITH GARLIC VINEGAR SAUCE

1   large head cauliflower, trimmed and separated into flowerets
    salt
    vegetable oil
    white pepper
½   cup flour
3   eggs, beaten
¾   cup fresh bread crumbs
6   tablespoons olive oil
2   garlic cloves, peeled
1   tablespoon paprika
2   tablespoons white vinegar
3   tablespoons boiling water

In a 3-quart saucepan cook cauliflower in lightly salted boiling water for 8 to 10 minutes. Drain on paper towels. In a deep fryer or saucepan heat 3 to 4 inches of oil to 350°. Sprinkle flowerets with salt and pepper, dip in flour and shake to remove excess. Dip in beaten egg and then bread crumbs. Fry in hot oil turning frequently for 4 minutes or until golden. Drain on paper towel and keep warm. In a small skillet heat olive oil over low heat. Drop in garlic cloves, cook 3 minutes and then remove with a slotted spoon. Discard garlic. Add paprika, vinegar and water to oil and cook for another minute. Pour sauce evenly over cauliflower.

Serves 6

MICROWAVE CAULIFLOWER WITH TANGY MUSTARD-CHEESE SAUCE

1   medium head cauliflower
½   cup mayonnaise
1   teaspoon minced onion
1   teaspoon prepared mustard
¾   cup grated Cheddar cheese

Core, wash and wrap cauliflower in waxed paper. Place in microwave oven and cook on full power 7 to 10 minutes or until cauliflower is tender but crisp. Do not overcook. Place cauliflower in a microwave-safe serving dish. Combine mayonnaise, onion and mustard. Spoon mixture over cauliflower and sprinkle with cheese. Cook an additional 1½ to 2 minutes on medium power or until topping is heated and cheese has melted.

Serves 4 to 6

SUPER SUMMER SUPPER

Dolma

Grilled Lemon Chicken

Cactus Caviar

Chilled Pea Salad

Chunie's Butterscotch Brownies

Mint Frosted Brownies

Assorted Fresh Fruit

Soft Drinks   Beer

Created by Hoover Dam, Lake Mead provides a variety of year-round activities including boating, water skiing, scuba diving and fishing. Southern Nevadans frequent its sunny beaches to relax with good friends and good food.

Tableware courtesy of Goldwaters Department Store

FRENCH FRIED ONION RINGS

These light, crisp fried onion rings make an appetizing snack as well as a tasty topping for broiled meats.

3	large onions, peeled
	milk
2	cups flour
¾	teaspoon garlic powder
1	teaspoon paprika
2	teaspoons salt
1	teaspoon pepper
3	dashes Tabasco
	oil for deep frying

Slice onions ¼-inch thick and separate into rings. Place slices in a large bowl and cover with milk. In another bowl combine flour with seasonings. In a deep fat fryer heat oil to 365°. One by one dip soaked onion rings in seasoned flour mixture. Deep fry 2 to 3 minutes or until golden crispy. Drain on brown paper and serve.

Serves 4 to 6

SAVORY ONIONS

16	small white boiling onions
½	cup butter or margarine
½	cup hot beef broth
	salt
	white pepper
	nutmeg
½	cup freshly grated Parmesan cheese

To remove skins drop onions into boiling water for 1 minute and then plunge into cold water. Peel. Cut an "X" in the root end of each onion. In a large skillet brown the onions in ¼ cup of the butter. Remove to a greased ovenproof casserole. Melt remaining butter and pour over onions. Add the broth and season with salt, pepper and nutmeg. Cover and bake in a preheated 325° oven approximately 25 to 35 minutes or until tender. Remove from oven, sprinkle with Parmesan cheese and serve.

Serves 4

ZUCCHINI CASSEROLE

6   cups sliced zucchini
2   eggs, separated
1   tablespoon flour
1   cup sour cream
    salt
1½ cups grated Cheddar cheese
6   slices bacon, cooked and
    crumbled
1   tablespoon butter
¼   cup dry bread crumbs

Cook zucchini in boiling water until tender, but slightly crisp. Drain. In a small bowl beat egg whites until stiff. Set aside. In a separate bowl combine egg yolks and flour, mixing well. Blend in sour cream and fold in egg whites. Layer half the zucchini in the bottom of an ovenproof baking dish and salt lightly. Pour half the sour cream mixture over the zucchini and then sprinkle half of the grated cheese and half of the crumbled bacon over all. Repeat the layering process. Melt the butter and stir in bread crumbs. Sprinkle on top of casserole. Bake in a preheated 350° oven 20 to 25 minutes.

Serves 6 to 8

Fresh fruits and vegetables look just as attractive on a table as flowers. You can decorate with ingredients—lemons or green peppers, for example—from one of the recipes you are serving.

ONION-ZUCCHINI AU GRATIN

3 cups peeled and sliced yellow onions
3 cups thinly sliced zucchini
4 tablespoons butter or margarine
2 eggs, beaten
¼ cup milk
1 teaspoon salt
⅛ teaspoon pepper
½ teaspoon dry mustard
1 cup grated Swiss cheese

In a large skillet sauté onion slices and zucchini in the butter until tender. Place in a shallow 1½-quart baking dish. Combine eggs, milk, salt, pepper, mustard and half of the cheese. Pour over vegetables and sprinkle with the remaining Swiss cheese. Bake in a preheated 375° oven for 20 minutes or until firm. For a moister consistency, add an additional egg and more milk.

Serves 6 to 8

CHEESE AND SPINACH BAKE

The quantities in this recipe should serve 12; but we doubt you'll have any left over even if your guest list is smaller.

2 10-ounce packages frozen spinach, thawed and drained
6 eggs, beaten
5 tablespoons flour
½ pound Monterey Jack cheese, shredded
2 pounds small curd cottage cheese
½ pound Cheddar cheese, shredded
½ cup butter or margarine, melted

In a large bowl combine all ingredients and mix well. Place in a greased 9 × 13-inch ovenproof casserole and bake in a preheated 350° oven for one hour. Serve immediately.

Serves 12

RATATOUILLE CREPES

Ratatouille is prized for its versatility. You may serve it hot or cold, or as an accompaniment to a brunch, luncheon or dinner entrée. One of the ways we like it best is as a filling for crepes.

1	large unpeeled eggplant, cubed
2	garlic cloves, minced
4	tablespoons olive oil
2	green peppers, cut in wide strips
4	tomatoes, quartered
2	shallots, chopped
¼	teaspoon dried basil
¼	teaspoon thyme
¼	teaspoon marjoram
	pinch rosemary
1	teaspoon salt
⅛	teaspoon pepper

In a large skillet over medium heat sauté eggplant and garlic in olive oil until soft. Add all remaining ingredients, cover skillet and reduce heat to low. Stir mixture occasionally to break down tomatoes. Cook vegetables until tender (about 45 minutes). Remove cover and cook an additional 25 to 30 minutes or until liquid has evaporated.

Makes filling for 12 crepes

ASSEMBLY

12	crepes (see Index)
	grated Swiss cheese

Fill each crepe with ¼ cup ratatouille. Roll filled crepes and place seam side down in a greased baking dish. Bake in a preheated 350° oven 15 minutes. Remove from oven, top with grated Swiss cheese and broil just until lightly brown.

CREAMED POTATO CASSEROLE

6   medium potatoes, peeled
4   tablespoons butter or
    margarine
1   medium onion, chopped
3   tablespoons chopped green
    pepper
2½ tablespoons flour
2   cups milk
1   tablespoon chopped pimiento
¾   cup grated sharp Cheddar
    cheese
    salt
    pepper

In a large saucepan cook potatoes until fork-tender. Drain and let cool. Dice potatoes and arrange in a greased 1½-quart ovenproof casserole. In a skillet melt butter and sauté onion and green pepper for 5 minutes. Blend in flour and stir in milk gradually, cooking until mixture thickens. Add pimiento and all but 2 tablespoons of the cheese. Mix well and add salt and pepper to taste. Pour sauce over the potatoes and sprinkle with the remaining 2 tablespoons of cheese. Bake in a preheated 350° oven for 30 minutes.

Serves 4 to 6

GERMAN POTATO PANCAKES

These potato pancakes are an excellent accompaniment to our Pork Roast with Mustard Sauce.

5   tablespoons flour
1½ pounds potatoes, peeled and
    grated
1   small onion, grated
1   egg, slightly beaten
1   teaspoon salt
½   teaspoon pepper
    vegetable oil for frying

In a large bowl combine flour, potatoes and onions. Toss lightly. Stir in the egg, salt and pepper. Lightly oil a large skillet and place over medium heat. Drop the potato batter by heaping tablespoons into the skillet. Fry until crisp and golden on both sides. Add more oil to the skillet as needed. Drain pancakes on paper towels.

Makes 16

SPINACH STUFFED POTATOES

The humble potato takes on "muscle" with the addition of spinach in this recipe.

4 baking potatoes
½ cup butter or margarine, softened
½ teaspoon salt
1 teaspoon sugar
¼ cup chopped chives
½ teaspoon dill weed
½ teaspoon garlic powder
1 10-ounce package frozen chopped spinach, cooked and drained
2 tablespoons sour cream
   Parmesan cheese

Bake potatoes and allow to cool. Cut potatoes in half lengthwise, remove pulp, and mash. Add butter, salt, sugar, chives, dill weed, garlic powder, spinach and sour cream to the mashed potatoes. Mix well. Fill potato skins with spinach mixture and place in an ovenproof dish. (Cover and chill if not baking immediately.) Bake uncovered in a preheated 350° oven for 30 minutes. Remove from oven and sprinkle with Parmesan cheese. Broil until golden brown on top.

Serves 6 to 8

GREEN CHILE STUFFED POTATOES

These potatoes can be prepared in advance and frozen if wrapped individually in heavy-duty aluminum foil. However, do not add the shredded cheese until ready to bake. Thaw, top with shredded cheese and bake 20 minutes.

6 large baking potatoes
½ cup butter or margarine, softened
1 cup sour cream
3 hard boiled eggs, chopped
1 4-ounce can diced green chiles
   salt
   shredded Longhorn-style Cheddar cheese

Bake potatoes until tender. Slice the tops off each potato and remove pulp to a large mixing bowl. Set aside shells. Mash potatoes adding the butter, sour cream, eggs, chiles and salt to taste. Fill the 6 reserved potato shells with the mixture. Top each potato with shredded cheese and bake in a preheated 350° oven for 15 minutes.

Serves 6

ORZO WITH PESTO

Using this rice-shaped pasta is an unusual variation to the traditional combination of pesto and linguini.

2   medium onions, chopped
2   carrots, peeled and thinly sliced
2   tablespoons butter
¾   cup dry white wine
¾   cup chicken broth
5   Italian plum tomatoes, coarsely chopped
1   cup fresh basil, tightly packed
½   cup olive oil
¼   cup freshly grated Parmesan cheese
¼   cup pine nuts
3   garlic cloves
      salt
      freshly ground pepper
1   pound orzo
⅓   cup chopped parsley

In a large skillet sauté onion and carrots in butter until onion is soft but not brown. Add wine and broth. Boil until slightly thickened. Add tomatoes and simmer 2 to 3 minutes. Prepare a pesto sauce by combining the fresh basil, olive oil, Parmesan cheese, nuts and garlic in a food processor or blender. Salt and pepper to taste and process to blend flavors. Set aside. Cook the orzo al dente. Drain well. Toss tomato mixture with orzo. Add pesto sauce and toss again. Garnish with parsley.

Serves 8 to 10

SAVORY STEWED APPLES

This is a lovely complement to almost any pork entrée.

2   pounds McIntosh apples (or similar variety), peeled and cored
4   tablespoons butter or margarine
½   cup sugar
2   tablespoons flour
½   cup water
½   cup white wine
1   small piece lemon rind
1   tablespoon lemon juice

Cut apples in thick slices. In a large skillet melt butter and sauté apple slices 2 to 3 minutes. Sprinkle with sugar and flour. Add water, wine, lemon rind and lemon juice. Bring mixture to a boil, cover and reduce heat. Simmer approximately 5 minutes or until apples are tender.

Serves 6

LEMON RICE

Lemon rice makes a nice co-star to our Parmesan Chicken.

1	cup chicken broth
1	cup water
2	tablespoons fresh lemon juice
½	teaspoon salt
1	cup long-grain rice
4	tablespoons butter or margarine
4	tablespoons minced parsley
1	teaspoon grated lemon rind

In a 3-quart saucepan combine broth, water, lemon juice and salt. Bring to a boil. Add rice and return to a boil. Cover and reduce heat to low. Cook rice for 18 to 20 minutes or until all water is absorbed. Remove rice from heat and add butter, parsley and lemon rind. Let stand for 5 minutes. Do not stir. Just before serving, fluff with a fork to blend.

Serves 4 to 6

FRIED RICE

2	eggs
½	teaspoon salt
6	tablespoons vegetable oil
4	cups cold cooked white rice
1	cup cooked and diced pork or beef
½	cup peas
2	tablespoons soy sauce
2	green onions, chopped

Beat eggs with salt. In a skillet heat oil and scramble eggs until firm. Remove skillet from heat. Finely chop cooked eggs. Add rice, meat and peas. Return skillet to stove and heat mixture through, breaking up any lumps of rice. Sprinkle soy sauce over all and garnish with chopped green onions.

Serves 4

GOLDEN RICE WITH SUNFLOWER SEEDS

3	tablespoons butter or margarine
½	cup chopped onion
1	cup long-grain rice
¼	teaspoon curry powder
2	cups chicken broth
1	cup finely chopped raw vegetables (such as celery, zucchini, broccoli)
⅓	cup raw sunflower seeds

In a large skillet melt butter and sauté onion. Add rice and cook 5 minutes. Add curry powder and chicken broth. Cover and simmer 20 minutes until rice is tender and liquid is absorbed. Add raw vegetables and seeds. Cook 3 to 4 minutes until vegetables are heated through.

Serves 6

WILD RICE WITH SAUTÉED VEGETABLES

5	cups chicken broth
1	cup wild rice
4	tablespoons butter
1	large onion, diced
2	red or green bell peppers, diced
15	large mushrooms, sliced

In a 4-quart saucepan combine chicken broth and rice. Bring contents to a boil, cover and reduce heat to low. Cook for 1½ to 2 hours or until rice is tender. Remove from heat and set aside. In a large skillet melt butter over medium heat and sauté onion until translucent. Add bell peppers and mushrooms. Cover and cook vegetables until tender but crisp. Drain any remaining liquid from the rice and stir in vegetables.

Serves 8 to 10

For a wild rice that is lighter and fuller in volume, we suggest the following preparation. (The flavor is not diminished.) In a large saucepan, cover rice with boiling water. Allow rice to soak until water has cooled. Drain off any excess liquid. Do this a total of 3 times. You can begin the process the evening before, soaking overnight.

Desserts

PAVLOVA

You may prepare the Pavlova using any seasonal fruit. Kiwi or a combination of kiwi and strawberries are two of our favorite variations.

MERINGUE

3	egg whites
¼	teaspoon cream of tartar
1	cup sugar

Beat egg whites until stiff, then slowly add cream of tartar and the sugar. Cut out a 9-inch circle of waxed paper and place on a cookie sheet. Spread meringue on waxed paper in a circle and using the back of a spoon, indent to make a bowl shape. Bake in a preheated 275° oven for 1 hour. Turn off oven but do not remove meringue until oven is cool.

LEMON FILLING

2	cups sifted powdered sugar
½	cup butter or margarine, softened
3	egg yolks
1	tablespoon fresh lemon juice
1	teaspoon grated lemon rind

In a mixing bowl cream the powdered sugar, butter and egg yolks. Beat until light and fluffy. Blend in lemon juice and lemon rind. Spread very carefully on top of the cooled meringue being careful not to crack the shell.

TOPPING

2	pints strawberries, hulled
1	cup heavy cream
4	tablespoons powdered sugar
1	teaspoon vanilla

Set aside 6 to 8 strawberries for garnish. Arrange the remaining strawberries on top of the lemon filling. Whip cream until stiff adding the powdered sugar and vanilla. Spread over the arranged berries. Garnish the Pavlova with reserved strawberries.

Serves 12

ENGLISH TOFFEE

1 cup crushed vanilla wafers (24 wafers)
1 cup chopped walnuts
½ cup butter
1 cup powdered sugar
3 eggs, separated
1½ ounces unsweetened chocolate, melted
½ teaspoon vanilla
whipped cream

Mix together the vanilla wafers and nuts. Firmly press half of this mixture in the bottom of a 9 × 9-inch pan. In a mixing bowl cream butter and sugar. Beat egg yolks and add with chocolate and vanilla to creamed mixture. Blend well. Beat egg whites until stiff and fold into batter. Pour over wafer crust and spread evenly. Top with remaining wafer-nut mixture and refrigerate overnight. Slice and serve with whipped cream.

Serves 10

FRENCH SILK SUPREME

In these times of health consciousness, there are those moments when nothing less than utter decadence will do. We present to you our gloriously rich French Silk Supreme.

8 ounces unsweetened chocolate
2 cups butter
3 cups sugar
4 teaspoons vanilla
8 eggs
2 packages ladyfingers
whipped cream
shaved chocolate

Melt chocolate and set aside to cool. In a large mixing bowl cream butter and sugar until pale yellow. Blend in cooled chocolate and vanilla. Beat in the eggs one at a time, allowing 5 to 7 minutes for each egg. Do not stop the machine. (Total beating time for eggs is 40 to 60 minutes.) Line the sides of a 9 or 10-inch springform pan with ladyfingers. Cut the remaining ladyfingers to fit the bottom of the pan. Pour the chocolate mixture into the pan and chill 4 hours or until set. Before serving, garnish with whipped cream rosettes and shaved chocolate.

Serves 12 to 16

MANDARIN DELIGHT

1 cup mandarin orange
  sections
½ cup Grand Marnier liqueur
1 tablespoon sugar
4 scoops vanilla ice cream,
  softened
4 scoops orange sherbet,
  softened
1 cup heavy cream, whipped

In a bowl toss oranges with Grand Marnier and sugar. Set aside. In a separate bowl mix ice cream and sherbet until well blended. Stir orange mixture into ice cream and divide among dessert dishes. Serve immediately topped with whipped cream.

Serves 4 to 6

RASPBERRY MERINGUE

MERINGUE

3 egg whites, room
  temperature
¾ cup sugar
1 cup finely chopped pecans
10 unsalted soda crackers, finely
  crushed

Beat egg whites until stiff. Add sugar and continue to beat. Fold in pecans and soda crackers. Butter a 10-inch pie plate and line with the meringue. Bake in a preheated 325° oven for approximately 25 minutes or until lightly brown. Cool shell.

FILLING

20 large marshmallows
½ cup orange juice
1 cup heavy cream, whipped
2 10-ounce packages frozen
  raspberries, thawed and
  drained

In the top of a double boiler melt the marshmallows. Remove from heat. Add orange juice and stir constantly until cool. Stir in the whipped cream and blend until smooth. Fold in raspberries. Pour mixture into shell and chill at least 3 to 4 hours. Cut into wedges and serve chilled.

Serves 8

ANGEL FOOD LEMON FLUFF

6   eggs, separated
1½ cups sugar
¾   cup lemon juice
1   teaspoon grated lemon rind
¼   teaspoon salt
1   envelope unflavored gelatin
¼   cup cold water
1   angel food cake

In the top of a double boiler combine the egg yolks, ¾ cup of the sugar, lemon juice, lemon rind and salt. Cook over hot water until slightly thickened. Soften gelatin in the cold water and add to the egg-lemon mixture. Mix well and refrigerate to cool. Beat egg whites until stiff, gradually adding the remaining ¾ cup sugar. Fold into the cooled lemon custard. Tear the angel food cake into pieces and fold into custard mixture. Pour into a lightly greased angel food cake pan. Chill 8 hours.

2   cups heavy cream
3   tablespoons sugar
1   teaspoon vanilla

Beat cream until stiff, gradually adding sugar and vanilla. Unmold chilled cake and frost with sweetened whipped cream. Refrigerate until ready to serve.

Serves 12

COLD LEMON SOUFFLÉ WITH RASPBERRY SAUCE

End the evening memorably. Feature our Cold Lemon Soufflé with Raspberry Sauce.

1   6-ounce package lemon jello
2   cups boiling water
2   7-ounce bottles lemon-lime soda
    grated rind of 1 lemon
    juice of one lemon
2   cups heavy cream, whipped
1   10-ounce package frozen raspberries
2   tablespoons raspberry jam

Stir jello into the boiling water until dissolved. Add the lemon-lime soda, lemon rind and lemon juice. Cool until thickened, then beat the mixture until foamy. Fold in whipped cream and turn into a 2-quart soufflé dish. Chill until firm. To prepare the sauce combine frozen raspberries and jam in a small saucepan. Heat through and serve warm over soufflé.

Serves 6 to 8

FROZEN ALMOND CHOCOLATE MOUSSE

For carefree entertaining, feature this show-off dessert from the freezer.

⅔ cup blanched whole almonds
½ cup graham cracker crumbs
3 tablespoons butter, melted
3 tablespoons sugar
1 pint vanilla or coffee ice cream, softened
6 ounces semi-sweet chocolate
2 large eggs, separated
3 tablespoons rum
1 cup heavy cream

Toast almonds in a 300° oven for 15 to 20 minutes. While almonds are warm, finely chop in a food processor or blender. Combine ⅓ cup of the chopped almonds with the graham cracker crumbs, melted butter and 1 tablespoon of the sugar. Press in an even layer in a greased 8-inch springform pan or round cake pan. Bake in a preheated 350° oven for 10 minutes. Cool and freeze crust. Spoon softened ice cream evenly over frozen crumb crust and return to freezer. In the top of a double boiler melt chocolate. Remove from heat. Next, beat egg yolks and slowly blend in the warm melted chocolate. Add rum and set aside. Beat egg whites until soft peaks form. Gradually beat in remaining 2 tablespoons of sugar. Set aside. In a separate mixing bowl whip ½ cup of the cream into soft peaks. Fold egg whites and then the whipped cream into the chocolate mixture. Reserve 2 tablespoons of the chopped almonds for garnish and fold remaining almonds into the chocolate. Pour the mousse over the ice cream, garnish with reserved almonds and freeze until firm. Whip remaining ½ cup of the heavy cream until stiff. Using a pastry tube decorate the top of the mousse with whipped cream rosettes. Cut in wedges to serve.

Serves 6

CHOCOLATE CHARLOTTE RUSSE

1   envelope unflavored gelatin
¾   cup cold water
3   ounces unsweetened
    chocolate
4   eggs, separated
¾   cup sugar
1   teaspoon vanilla
    salt
½   teaspoon cream of tartar
1   cup heavy cream, whipped
16 ladyfingers, split lengthwise
    toasted almonds

Soften gelatin in ¼ cup of the cold water. Over low heat melt chocolate in remaining ½ cup water, stirring constantly. Remove from heat, add softened gelatin and stir to dissolve. In a separate bowl beat the egg yolks until thick and lemon-colored. Gradually beat in ½ cup sugar. Add vanilla and a dash of salt. Slowly stir chocolate mixture into egg mixture. Cool to room temperature and then stir until smooth. Beat egg whites with cream of tartar to form soft peaks. Gradually add the remaining ¼ cup sugar and beat to stiff peaks. Fold beaten egg whites and then the whipped cream into chocolate mixture. Arrange split ladyfingers on the bottom and around the sides of a 9-inch springform pan. (You may need to cut ladyfingers to fit.) Fill with ½ of the chocolate mixture. Add another layer of split ladyfingers and then the remaining chocolate mixture. Sprinkle top with toasted almonds. Refrigerate 8 hours or until firm. Remove sides of pan before serving.

Serves 8 to 10

FANTASTIC FUDGE

Busy holiday bakers will appreciate this quick-to-prepare candy that utilizes microwave magic!

    butter or margarine
1   pound powdered sugar
½   cup cocoa
¼   cup milk
½   cup butter
1   teaspoon vanilla
¾   cup chopped pecans or
    walnuts

Butter an 8-inch square dish and set aside. In a large microwave-safe bowl sift sugar and cocoa together. Mix well. Add milk and butter, but do not stir. Place in a microwave oven and cook on full-power for 2½ minutes. Remove from microwave and stir just enough to combine ingredients. Quickly stir in vanilla and chopped nuts. Pour mixture into the buttered dish spreading evenly. Allow fudge to cool completely before cutting into squares.

Makes 16 to 20 pieces

IRRESISTIBLE ICE CREAM PIE

For a less rich pie use only half of the chocolate sauce. Freeze the remaining sauce for a second "irresistible" pie at a later date. This keeps well in the freezer—if it's hidden so no one can find it!

CRUST

32 Oreo cookies, finely crushed
⅓ cup melted butter

In a bowl combine crushed cookies and melted butter. Mix well and press into the bottom and 1-inch up the sides of a 10-inch springform pan. Bake crust in a preheated 350° oven for 10 minutes. Cool.

FILLING

1 quart coffee ice cream, slightly softened
1½ cups evaporated milk
⅓ cup butter
4 ounces unsweetened chocolate
1 cup sugar
1 cup heavy cream
½ cup Kahlúa liqueur
⅓ cup chopped pecans or walnuts

Press the ice cream into the cooled crust and freeze. In a small saucepan combine evaporated milk, butter, chocolate and sugar. Cook over medium heat stirring constantly until thickened (about 10 to 15 minutes). Cool sauce completely and then pour over ice cream spreading evenly. Freeze. Whip cream until stiff. Blend Kahlúa into cream and spread over frozen pie. Sprinkle with chopped nuts and freeze until solid. When ready to serve, remove springform sides and place on a serving platter.

Serves 16

Make family and guests feel like royalty with this elegant but easy option for serving after dinner coffee. Brew a very rich fragrant coffee and pour from your favorite pot. Accompany with small bowls of toppings, including crushed peppermint candies, grated semi-sweet chocolate and whipped cream. With coffee served this way in front of a blazing hearth, who would be interested in dessert?

CHOCOLATE LOVER'S HEAVEN

Lusciously rich and smooth, chocolate glorifies an occasion like nothing else. This recipe is our salute to chocolate lovers around the world. And if that isn't enough, it's simple and quick to prepare.

¾ cup milk
6 ounces semi-sweet chocolate chips
1 large egg
2 tablespoons sugar
2 tablespoons brandy
  whipped cream

Scald the milk. In a food processor combine the scalded milk, chocolate chips, egg, sugar and brandy. Cover and process 20 seconds or until smooth. The mixture will be thin. Pour into individual dessert cups or a small bowl. Chill for 3 hours or until dessert is set. Serve plain or with whipped cream.

Serves 4

SPICY CARROT CAKE

Of all the carrot cakes we tested—this one "hit the jackpot"!

2 cups flour
2 cups sugar
2 teaspoons baking soda
2 teaspoons salt
1 tablespoon cinnamon
3 cups peeled and grated carrots
4 eggs
1½ cups vegetable oil
1 cup chopped walnuts

Sift together flour, sugar, baking soda, salt and cinnamon. In a food processor or blender place 1 cup carrots, 1 egg and ½ cup oil. Process and add this mixture to dry ingredients. Repeat this procedure twice adding walnuts and the fourth egg during the last blending. (A large food processor can accommodate all of the carrots, eggs and oil in one processing.) Beat the combined ingredients until smooth. Pour into a greased bundt pan and bake in a preheated 350° oven for 1 hour. Cool and frost with cream cheese frosting.

CREAM CHEESE FROSTING

½ cup butter or margarine, softened
8 ounces cream cheese, softened
1 pound powdered sugar
1 teaspoon vanilla

Cream butter and cheese together. Beat in powdered sugar and vanilla until smooth. Spread on cake.

Serves 12

APPLE CAKE

½ cup vegetable oil
2 cups packed brown sugar
4 cups peeled, cored and
   chopped apples
1 cup chopped pecans or
   walnuts
2 eggs, beaten
2 teaspoons vanilla
2 cups flour
2 teaspoons baking soda
½ teaspoon salt
1 teaspoon cinnamon
1 teaspoon nutmeg

In a large mixing bowl pour oil and sugar over apples. Add nuts, eggs and vanilla. Set aside. Sift together flour, baking soda, salt, cinnamon and nutmeg. Add to apples. Mix until all ingredients are moistened. Pour batter into a greased and lightly floured 9 × 13-inch pan. Bake in a preheated 350° oven for 40 to 45 minutes or until done. Cool and refrigerate for at least one day. Dust lightly with powdered sugar, or frost with sour cream icing. To serve, cut into squares.

SOUR CREAM ICING

½ cup sour cream
1 cup sugar
½ teaspoon baking soda

In a small saucepan over medium heat combine all ingredients. Bring to a boil stirring frequently. Remove from heat, cool slightly and pour over cake.

Serves 12 to 14

HOT MILK CAKE

One of our testers thought this cake tasted even better the second day.

2   cups flour
    pinch of salt
4   teaspoons baking powder
4   eggs
2   cups sugar
4   tablespoons butter or
    margarine, softened
1   cup hot milk
1   teaspoon vanilla

Sift together the flour, salt and baking powder. Set aside. In a large mixing bowl beat eggs for two minutes. Add sugar and beat until light and fluffy. Add flour mixture, butter and hot milk. Beat well. Stir in vanilla. Pour batter into 2 greased 9-inch cake pans which have been lined with waxed paper. Bake in a preheated 350° oven for 25 minutes or until cake tests done. Cool and remove from pans.

LEMON FILLING

5   tablespoons flour
1   cup sugar
1   cup boiling water
1   egg yolk
¼   cup lemon juice
    grated rind of 1 lemon

Combine flour and sugar in small saucepan. Add boiling water and cook slowly until mixture thickens. Add egg yolk, lemon juice and rind. Stir well. Remove from heat and cool. Spread cooled filling between cake layers.

FROSTING

2   cups heavy cream
2   tablespoons sugar

Frost with cream which has been stiffly whipped with 2 tablespoons sugar.

Serves 8 to 12

PRUNE CAKE

This is an exceptionally moist cake and keeps well.

2   cups flour
1   teaspoon baking soda
1   teaspoon salt
1   teaspoon nutmeg
1   teaspoon cinnamon
¼   teaspoon allspice
2   cups sugar
1   cup vegetable oil
3   eggs
1   teaspoon vanilla
1   cup buttermilk
1   cup chopped pecans
1   cup chopped prunes

In a large mixing bowl sift together flour, baking soda, salt, nutmeg, cinnamon and allspice. Add sugar, oil, eggs, vanilla and buttermilk. Beat until smooth. Stir in nuts and prunes. Pour into a greased and lightly floured 9 × 13-inch pan and bake in a preheated 350° oven for 1 hour or until cake tests done.

GLAZE

1   cup sugar
½   cup butter or margarine
1   cup buttermilk
1   teaspoon baking soda
    whipped cream

During the last 5 minutes of baking prepare glaze by combining sugar, butter, buttermilk and baking soda in saucepan. Bring to a rolling boil. Remove cake from oven. Poke holes in the top of the cake with a fork. Pour glaze mixture over cake while both are hot. Cool. Serve with whipped cream.

Serves 12

RICH RICH CHEESECAKE

CRUST

1⅓ cups graham cracker crumbs
¼ cup sugar
½ cup butter or margarine, melted

In a bowl combine cracker crumbs, sugar and butter. Mix well and press into the bottom of a 9-inch springform pan. Chill.

CHEESE FILLING

24 ounces cream cheese, softened
1½ cups sugar
⅛ teaspoon salt
4 eggs
1 teaspoon vanilla

In a mixing bowl beat cream cheese, sugar and salt until fluffy. Add eggs one at a time beating well after each addition. Beat in vanilla and pour batter into crumb crust. Bake in a preheated 350° oven for 50 minutes or until firm in center. Remove from oven and let rest for 15 minutes. Increase oven temperature to 450°.

TOPPING

2 cups sour cream
¼ cup sugar
1 teaspoon vanilla

Combine sour cream, sugar and vanilla in a small bowl. Mix well. Gently spread over cheesecake and return to oven for 10 minutes or until topping is set. Cool cake on wire rack and then refrigerate. When ready to serve, remove the sides of the springform pan and place the cheesecake on a platter.

Serves 12

MINT FROSTED BROWNIES

For party appeal the mint frosting can be tinted green or pink using food coloring.

½   cup butter or margarine, softened
1   cup sugar
1   teaspoon vanilla
2   eggs
2   ounces unsweetened chocolate, melted
½   cup flour
½   cup chopped nuts

In a mixing bowl combine butter, sugar, vanilla, eggs and chocolate. Beat well. Stir in flour and nuts. Pour into a greased 8 × 8-inch pan and bake in a preheated 375° oven for 25 minutes or until brownies test done. Remove from oven and cool.

MINT FROSTING

2   tablespoons butter, melted
1   cup powdered sugar
1   tablespoon milk
½   teaspoon peppermint extract

Combine butter, powdered sugar, milk and peppermint extract. Stir until smooth. Frost brownies.

CHOCOLATE GLAZE

2   tablespoons butter
2   ounces unsweetened chocolate

In a small saucepan over low heat, melt 2 tablespoons butter. Add the unsweetened chocolate and stir to melt. Mix until smooth. When mint frosting has set, drizzle glaze over all.

Makes 1½ dozen

MEGAN'S MOUNTAIN MEADOW BIRTHDAY

Fruit Crush

Thin Crust Homemade Pizza

Caramel Crunch

Miniature Party Cupcakes

Nearby Spring Mountain Ranch is just the spot for this children's birthday party. Prior to being dedicated a State Park in 1975, its picturesque home and surrounding meadows were owned by Lum of radio's famous Lum and Abner comedy team, the millionairess Vera Krupp of the German munitions family, and subsequently Howard Hughes. Today community volunteers and park employees continue guided tours and arts in the park programs initiated by the Junior League of Las Vegas and the Nevada Division of State Parks. The park's Visitor Center offers information on tours and current programs.

Tableware and accessories furnished by Bullock's Department Store

FROSTED BANANA SPICE COOKIES

½ cup vegetable shortening
1 cup packed brown sugar
2 eggs
1 cup mashed ripe bananas
 (approximately 2)
2 cups flour
2 teaspoons baking powder
¼ teaspoon baking soda
¼ teaspoon salt
½ teaspoon cinnamon
¼ teaspoon ground cloves
½ cup chopped nuts

In a mixing bowl beat together shortening, sugar, eggs and bananas. Stir in all remaining ingredients. Cover batter and chill 1 hour. Drop dough by teaspoonfuls at least 2 inches apart onto a lightly greased cookie sheet. Bake on the middle rack of a preheated 375° oven about 8 to 10 minutes. Allow to cool before frosting.

LEMON BUTTER ICING

½ cup butter or margarine,
 softened
3 cups powdered sugar
2 tablespoons lemon juice
½ teaspoon grated lemon rind

In a mixing bowl cream butter and sugar. Beat in lemon juice and rind. Continue beating until smooth and of spreading consistency.

Makes 3 dozen

FRENCH LACE COOKIES

These taste-tempting treats are extremely fragile. If any should break, save and use as a crumbled topping for ice cream.

½ cup butter
1 cup sugar
½ teaspoon salt
1 cup oatmeal (quick or
 regular)
1 egg
¼ teaspoon baking powder
3 tablespoons flour
1 teaspoon vanilla
¼ cup flaked coconut

In a 3-quart saucepan melt butter. Remove from heat and add all remaining ingredients. Batter will be runny. Cover cookie sheets with aluminum foil. Drop batter by teaspoonfuls at least 3 inches apart onto cookie sheets. Bake in a preheated 375° oven 8 to 10 minutes. Watch cookies carefully as they burn easily. Remove from oven and leave on foil until cool. Peel off foil.

Makes 3 dozen

CHOCOLATE CHOCOLATE CHIP COOKIES

What would a cookbook be without a chocolate chip cookie recipe! We think this one is a winner.

1¾ cups flour
¼ teaspoon baking soda
1 cup butter or margarine, softened
1 teaspoon vanilla
1 cup sugar
½ cup packed dark brown sugar
1 egg
⅓ cup unsweetened cocoa
2 tablespoons milk
1 cup chopped pecans or walnuts
6 ounces semi-sweet chocolate chips

Stir together flour and baking soda. Set aside. Using an electric mixer cream butter. Add vanilla and sugars and beat until fluffy. Beat in egg. At low speed beat in cocoa, then milk. With a wooden spoon mix in flour just until blended. Stir in nuts and chocolate chips. Drop by rounded teaspoonfuls onto non-stick or foil lined cookie sheets. Bake in a preheated 350° oven for 12 to 13 minutes. Remove from oven and cool slightly before removing from cookie sheets.

Makes 3 dozen

DATE TICKLES

1 cup flour
1 teaspoon baking powder
½ cup maraschino cherries, diced
1 cup chopped nuts
1 cup chopped dates
3 egg whites
1 cup powdered sugar
½ teaspoon salt
1 teaspoon vanilla

In a bowl combine flour and baking powder. Dredge cherries, nuts and dates in the flour mixture. Set aside. Beat egg whites until soft peaks form. Gradually add sugar, salt and vanilla until stiff peaks form. Fold in cherries, nuts, dates and flour remaining in the bowl. Spread mixture in a greased and floured 6 × 10-inch pan. Bake in a preheated 325° oven until lightly golden, approximately 12 minutes. Be careful not to overbake. While still warm cut into 1 × 2-inch cookies. Store in an air-tight canister.

Makes 30

CHUNIE'S BUTTERSCOTCH BROWNIES

½ cup butter or margarine
2 cups packed brown sugar
2 eggs
1 cup flour
2 teaspoons baking powder
1 teaspoon salt
1 teaspoon vanilla
6 ounces semi-sweet chocolate chips

In a 3-quart saucepan melt butter over low heat. Remove from heat and stir in brown sugar and eggs. Add flour, baking powder, salt and vanilla. Mix well. Stir in chocolate chips and spread batter into a greased 9 × 13-inch pan. Bake in a preheated 350° oven 25 minutes. Cool. Cut into squares.

Makes 2 dozen

CASHEW COOKIES

½ cup butter or margarine
1 cup packed brown sugar
1 egg
½ teaspoon vanilla
2 cups flour
¾ teaspoon baking powder
¾ teaspoon baking soda
¼ teaspoon salt
½ cup sour cream
2 cups cashew halves or pieces

In a large mixing bowl cream butter and sugar. Beat in egg and then vanilla. Sift together the flour, baking powder, baking soda and salt. Add to the creamed mixture and beat thoroughly. Beat in sour cream. Stir in cashews. Drop by teaspoonfuls on greased cookie sheets. Bake in a preheated 400° oven for 10 minutes. When almost cool, frost with coffee icing.

COFFEE ICING

4 tablespoons butter or margarine
3 tablespoons brewed coffee
¼ teaspoon vanilla
2 cups powdered sugar

In a large saucepan melt butter. Remove from heat and add coffee, vanilla and sugar. Mix well. Frost cookies.

Makes 4 to 5 dozen

VINEGAR PIE CRUST

1   teaspoon white vinegar
1   egg, beaten
6   tablespoons water
1   teaspoon salt
3   cups flour
1   cup plus 2 tablespoons
    vegetable shortening

In a bowl combine vinegar and egg. Blend well. Add water and salt. Set aside. Place flour in a large bowl. Cut the shortening into the flour until small balls form. Add the liquid ingredients. Mix well. Divide dough into 3 equal size portions. Roll each portion out on a floured board or between sheets of waxed paper and transfer to individual pie plates. If you need only one pie crust, tightly wrap remaining pastry and freeze for later use.

Makes 3 9-inch pastry shells

ONE HUNDRED YEAR OLD PIE CRUST

The texture of this crust is light and flaky. Both testers of this recipe have vowed that this is the crust recipe they will use from now on!

4   cups flour
1   teaspoon salt
2   cups vegetable shortening
1   cup water

Into a large bowl sift the flour with the salt. Using a pastry blender cut the shortening into the flour until small balls form. Add the water and toss gently with a fork. Handle as little as possible! Dough will be wet. Wrap in foil and refrigerate for at least 6 hours. It may be refrigerated up to 4 weeks if tightly wrapped. When ready to use, remove only the amount of dough needed. Roll on a well-floured board and place in pie plate.

Makes 4 10-inch pastry shells

SKY-HIGH LEMON PIE

Here is an option for an imposing dessert that will score "21" at your table. Increase the number of egg whites to 8 in this meringue to make it puff "sky-high."

1	9-inch pastry shell, baked and cooled
1	cup sugar
¼	cup flour
	dash of salt
1	cup water
3	egg yolks
2	tablespoons butter or margarine, softened
¼	cup lemon juice

In a mixing bowl combine sugar, flour, salt and ¼ cup of the water. Beat until smooth. In a separate bowl beat egg yolks with the remaining ¾ cup water. In the top of a double boiler combine sugar mixture and egg mixture. Cook, stirring constantly until thick. Cover and simmer an additional 10 minutes. Thoroughly blend in the butter and lemon juice. Pour filling into baked pastry shell.

MERINGUE

3	egg whites
½	teaspoon salt
9	tablespoons sugar

Beat the egg whites until stiff, but not dry. Add salt and gradually add sugar while continuing to beat. Swirl meringue on top of filling and bake in a preheated 325° oven for 20 minutes. Remove from oven and cool before serving.

Serves 6

Lemons and limes at room temperature will release a larger volume of juice when squeezed.

BROWN BAG APPLE CRUMB PIE

If you want this unusual method of "brown bagging" your apple pie to really work, don't peek during the cooking process.

1	9-inch pastry shell, unbaked
1½	cups sugar
1	teaspoon cinnamon
½	teaspoon nutmeg
5	tablespoons flour
8	tart apples, peeled, cored and sliced

In a large bowl combine sugar, cinnamon, nutmeg and flour. Toss apple slices in this mixture and place in pastry shell.

TOPPING

½	cup packed brown sugar
¼	teaspoon cinnamon
2	tablespoons flour
⅛	teaspoon salt
2	tablespoons butter or margarine
½	cup chopped walnuts or pecans

Combine the brown sugar, cinnamon, flour and salt. Cut butter into dry ingredients with a pastry blender until crumbly. Stir in nuts and spread the mixture evenly over the top of the apples. Place the pie in a brown grocery bag and staple shut. Bake in a preheated 350° oven for 1½ hours. (No, the bag won't burn.)

Serves 8

MINIATURE PARTY CUPCAKES

Kids ages 2 to 62 love this sweet treat—so does the hostess because they can be made in advance of the party and frozen until ready to enjoy.

1½	cups sifted cake flour
1⅓	cups sugar
¼	cup cocoa
1	tablespoon white vinegar
1	teaspoon vanilla
1	teaspoon baking soda
½	teaspoon salt
⅓	cup vegetable oil
1	cup water
8	ounces cream cheese, softened
1	egg
6	ounces semi-sweet chocolate chips
	powdered sugar

In a mixing bowl combine flour, 1 cup of the sugar, cocoa, vinegar, vanilla, baking soda, salt, oil and water. Mix well and set aside. In another bowl combine cream cheese, egg and remaining ⅓ cup sugar. Cream well and fold in the chocolate chips. Line 48 miniature muffin cups with paper liners. Fill each cup ⅓ full with the cocoa batter and top with one teaspoon of the cheese-chocolate chip mixture. Bake in a preheated 350° oven for 25 minutes. When cool dust tops with powdered sugar.

Makes 4 dozen

SHORTBREAD WITH STRAWBERRIES AND CREAM

Simple ways are often the best when it comes to enjoying the goodness of fresh strawberries. With very little effort you can create this taste-tempting dessert.

1	cup butter, softened
2	cups flour
⅔	cup sugar
1	egg yolk
	strawberries
	whipped cream

Cream butter, flour and sugar. Add egg yolk and mix well. In a 10-inch pie plate pat the dough to a thickness of ½-inch on the bottom and up the sides. Flute the edges with a fork. Bake in a preheated 350° oven for 15 minutes. Reduce oven temperature to 300°. Bake for 30 minutes or until golden brown. Cut into wedges and serve with fresh sliced strawberries and freshly whipped cream.

Serves 4

LUSCIOUS LEMON TARTS

TART SHELLS

1 cup flour
¼ cup sugar
⅛ teaspoon salt
½ cup butter
1 egg yolk
½ teaspoon almond extract

Sift flour, sugar and salt into a bowl. Add butter, egg yolk and almond extract. Using your hands mix dough thoroughly. Turn dough out onto a floured board and knead until smooth. Wrap in plastic wrap and chill for approximately 1 hour. To form tart shells pinch off pieces of dough and press into buttered tart tins. Do not extend dough above rim. Bake in a preheated 400° oven for 8 to 10 minutes or until golden. Allow shells to cool only 5 minutes before unmolding. To unmold, invert muffin tin on a flat surface. Tap gently to release tart shells.

FILLING

½ cup butter
1½ cups sugar
2 teaspoons grated lemon rind
½ cup fresh lemon juice
1 teaspoon cornstarch
3 eggs
3 egg yolks

In the top of a double boiler combine butter, sugar, lemon rind, lemon juice and cornstarch. Stirring frequently, heat mixture until butter has melted and sugar is dissolved (approximately 5 minutes). In a small mixing bowl beat together the 3 eggs and 3 egg yolks until they are thick and a ribbon forms from the end of a spoon. Add eggs to lemon mixture and cook until very thick. Stir constantly with a wire whisk. Fill tart shells and refrigerate at least 4 hours before serving.

Makes 18 miniature or 12 2½-inch shells

AMARETTO ICE

Coping with summer heat is a way of life in the Southwest. Enjoying a serving of Amaretto Ice is one of our ways to beat the heat. To allow adequate time for freezing this recipe, it is probably best to prepare it one day in advance.

2   cups water
¾   cup sugar
1   teaspoon grated lemon rind
    juice of 1 lemon
½   cup Amaretto liqueur
2   egg whites

In a small saucepan combine water and sugar. Bring to a boil and boil for 5 minutes. Remove from heat and add lemon rind, juice of one lemon and Amaretto. Freeze this mixture until slushy. Remove from freezer and beat until smooth. Beat egg whites until stiff. Fold into Amaretto mixture and refreeze until firm. Serve in chilled sherbet glasses.

Serves 6

"SURE BET" LEMON SHERBET

For a "frosty" presentation chill sherbet glasses before filling. Garnish with a sprig of fresh mint or fresh blueberries.

1½ cups sugar
1⅓ cups milk
    juice of 2 lemons
    finely grated rind of 1 lemon
1   egg, beaten
1   cup heavy cream

In a large bowl combine sugar and milk. Stir until sugar is dissolved. Add the lemon juice, grated rind and beaten egg blending well. In a separate bowl beat cream until it holds soft peaks. Fold into the lemon mixture, blending well. Pour the mixture into ice cube trays or a 9 × 9-inch pan. Freeze until almost firm, about 4 to 6 hours. Turn into a bowl and beat until smooth. Cover and return to freezer until firm.

Makes 1½ quarts

CRÈME DE MENTHE DREAM

We have given you one combination of ice cream and liqueur. You can easily substitute other flavors of ice cream and liqueur to come up with your own "winning" combination.

2 cups finely crushed chocolate wafer crumbs
5⅓ tablespoons butter or margarine, softened
½ gallon vanilla ice cream
6 tablespoons green crème de menthe liqueur

In a bowl combine wafer crumbs and butter. Mix well and press into the bottom of a 10-inch springform pan. Chill crust in freezer for 30 minutes. Soften ice cream in a large bowl. When soft, stir in the crème de menthe thoroughly. Pour mixture into the chilled crust and freeze for at least 3 hours.

TOPPING

3 ounces unsweetened chocolate
½ cup water
¾ cup sugar
¼ teaspoon salt
4½ tablespoons butter, cubed
½ teaspoon vanilla

In the top of a double boiler combine chocolate and water. Melt the chocolate over low heat stirring occasionally. Add the sugar and salt. Continue cooking, stirring constantly, until the sugar has dissolved and sauce has thickened slightly. Remove from heat and stir in butter and vanilla. Cool thoroughly and then drizzle over the frozen pie. Freeze until firm.

Serves 8 to 10

PECAN PRALINE SAUCE

1 tablespoon butter
½ cup buttermilk
1 cup sugar
¾ cup chopped pecans
½ teaspoon baking soda
    vanilla ice cream

In a heavy saucepan or the top of a double boiler, melt butter over low heat. Add the buttermilk, sugar, pecans and baking soda. Stir over low heat until slightly thickened. Serve warm over vanilla ice cream.

Makes 1¼ cups

CHANTILLY-RUM SAUCE FOR FRESH FRUIT

Your guests will be asking for "encores" when you fold fresh strawberries into our Chantilly-Rum Sauce and serve from your favorite crystal bowl. You may also serve the sauce as a dip with a variety of fresh fruit.

½ teaspoon unflavored gelatin
5 tablespoons cold water
¼ cup egg whites
   (approximately 2 eggs)
1 cup sugar
¼ teaspoon cream of tartar
⅛ teaspoon salt
½ teaspoon vanilla
2 tablespoons Myers's rum
1 cup heavy cream

In a small heat-proof dish combine gelatin with 2 tablespoons of the cold water. Allow to stand until thick. In the upper part of a double boiler combine egg whites, sugar, cream of tartar, salt, vanilla and remaining 3 tablespoons cold water. Mix well with a wooden spoon. Bring water in lower part of a double boiler to a boil, place this upper part in position and reduce heat to low. Using an electric mixer on high speed, beat until mixture is thick and clings to pan. Remove top of boiler from water and set aside. Place dish of thickened gelatin in the simmering water. When thinned, stir in rum gently and remove dish from water. Add gelatin-rum mixture a little at a time to sauce. Beat only until well blended. Refrigerate about 1 to 1½ hours to cool and thicken slightly. In a large mixing bowl whip cream until it holds soft peaks. Slowly fold cooled rum mixture into the whipped cream. Blend well. Refrigerate sauce until ready to serve. (It will hold up to 2 days.) Stir briefly before serving to insure smoothness.

Makes 2 cups

Holiday Potpourri

HOT MULLED CIDER

The fragrance of this seasonal beverage steeping in the kitchen is as delightfully warming as its flavor.

2 quarts apple cider
½ cup packed brown sugar
1 teaspoon whole allspice
1½ teaspoons whole cloves
2 cinnamon sticks
1 orange, sliced

Combine all ingredients in a crockpot. Cook at high temperature for 1 hour and then reduce temperature to low setting. Simmer for 2 hours.

Makes 2 quarts

EGG NOG

6 eggs, separated
⅛ teaspoon salt
½ cup sugar
1 cup brandy or bourbon
2 cups heavy cream
2 cups milk
nutmeg

In a bowl beat egg whites and salt until stiff peaks form. Set aside. In a larger bowl beat egg yolks until light. Beating constantly, gradually add sugar and then the brandy, cream and milk. When well mixed fold in egg whites. To serve, ladle into mugs or punch cups and sprinkle with nutmeg.

Serves 8

POMEGRANATE CORDIAL

We feature the juice of the pomegranate in this recipe because of its ruby red holiday color and because the fruit is locally abundant at this time of year. However, you may substitute almost any clarified fruit juice.

2 cups clarified pomegranate juice
2 cups vodka
2 cups sugar

Combine all ingredients in a closed lid jar. Store at room temperature and shake well every day for two weeks. The cordial may be served chilled or at room temperature.

Makes 1 quart

CRANBERRY PUNCH

The zesty flavor of this eye-appealing, colorful punch, is one of the ways to celebrate the joy of the season.

4 cups cranberries
4 cups sugar
2 cups water
2 cinnamon sticks
12 whole cloves
4 cups pineapple juice
2 cups fresh lemon juice
2 quarts ginger ale, chilled
2 quarts club soda, chilled

In a 4-quart saucepan combine cranberries, sugar, water, cinnamon sticks and cloves. Stirring, heat mixture to a boil. Reduce heat to simmer and continue to cook until cranberries are tender. Allow mixture to cool and then strain through a sieve or a double layer of cheese cloth. Add the pineapple and lemon juices to the strained liquid. Freeze for at least 24 hours. When ready to serve, place frozen punch in a large punch bowl. Stir in ginger ale and club soda.

Serves 30

WASSAIL PUNCH

The word "wassail" is derived from the old Anglo-Saxon drinking pledge "Wass-Hael" which meant "be in health." It was the custom to toast the lord of the manor, and the practice was easily assimilated into the Christmas tradition. Our recipe for this seasonal beverage is a direct import from England.

1 gallon apple cider or apple juice
1 12-ounce can frozen orange juice concentrate
1½ cups water
1 6-ounce can lemonade concentrate
16 whole cloves
4 cinnamon sticks
1 teaspoon nutmeg
1 teaspoon ground cinnamon
1 teaspoon ground cloves
2 cups bourbon
1 orange, sliced
1 lemon, sliced

In a large pot combine all ingredients except orange and lemon slices. Heat mixture to boiling, then reduce heat to simmer. Simmer for 10 minutes to blend flavors. To serve, float orange and lemon slices on top.

Serves 40

POMEGRANATE MOLDED SALAD

This is a colorful salad for fall and winter entertaining. Pomegranates are native to the climate of the desert Southwest with harvest beginning around the middle of October. Although not grown for commercial distribution, Southern Nevadans enjoy an abundance of this somewhat unusual fruit.

1   6-ounce package raspberry jello
2   cups hot water
3   ounces cream cheese, softened
2   cups cold water
2   cups heavy cream, whipped to stiff peaks
3   pomegranates, cracked and seeded

In a large bowl dissolve jello in hot water. Add cream cheese and cold water. Mix well. When mixture begins to thicken fold in whipped cream and pomegranate seeds. Pour into a mold and refrigerate overnight or until firm.

Serves 6

CRANBERRY CHUTNEY

Bottled in gift-size jars, our Cranberry Chutney makes a nice holiday remembrance. Give a jar to your best friend for her holiday table.

4   cups cranberries
1   cup seedless raisins
1⅔ cups sugar
1½ teaspoons ground ginger
¼   teaspoon ground cloves
1   tablespoon ground cinnamon
1   cup water
1   medium onion, chopped
1   medium apple, peeled, cored and diced
½   cup diced celery

In a large saucepan combine cranberries, raisins, sugar, ginger, cloves, cinnamon and water. Cook over medium heat for 15 minutes. Add the onion, apple and celery. Cook an additional 15 minutes. Cool and refrigerate. The chutney may also be frozen for use at a later date.

Makes 4 cups

POMEGRANATE - RASPBERRY JELLY

If fresh pomegranates are not available, you can purchase the juice in health food stores.

2 cups clarified pomegranate juice (approximately 6 to 8 pomegranates)
2 cups frozen raspberries
¼ cup lemon juice
1 package dry pectin
7½ cups sugar

Combine pomegranate juice, raspberries and lemon juice in a 4-quart saucepan. Add the dry pectin. Bring mixture to a boil over high heat stirring constantly. Immediately blend in sugar and continue to boil for 2 minutes. Remove saucepan from heat and skim off foam. Pour into hot sterile jars and seal according to the pectin package directions.

Makes 5 to 6 pints

ITALIAN ANISE COOKIES

2 cups sugar
1 cup butter, melted
4 tablespoons anise seed
4 tablespoons anisette or other anise-flavored liqueur
3 tablespoons whiskey (2 teaspoons vanilla mixed with 2 teaspoons water may be substituted)
2 cups coarsely chopped almonds or walnuts
2 tablespoons pine nuts (optional)
6 eggs
3½ cups flour
1 tablespoon baking powder

In a large mixing bowl beat together sugar and butter. Add anise seed, anisette, whiskey and nuts. Mix well. Beat in eggs. Combine flour and baking powder and stir into the sugar mixture. Cover and chill batter 2 to 3 hours. Grease 2 baking sheets. Flour hands and divide dough into fourths. Roll each quarter into a roll the length of the baking sheet. Shape the rolls to form flat loaves about ½-inch thick and 2-inches wide. Place 2 loaves on each sheet parallel and well apart. Keep flouring hands if dough is sticky. Bake in a preheated 375° oven for 20 minutes. Remove from oven and cool loaves only long enough so that you can touch them. Cut into diagonal slices about ½ to ¾-inch thick. Arrange slices, cut side down, on baking sheet. Return to oven and bake for an additional 15 minutes or until lightly toasted. Do not overbake. Cool on wire racks and store in air-tight containers.

Makes 9 dozen

NUTCUPS

3   ounces cream cheese, softened
½   cup butter, softened
1   cup flour

In a bowl combine cream cheese, butter and flour. Using your hands mix thoroughly and roll into 24 small balls. Refrigerate at least 1 hour or overnight. When ready to bake put each ball into a 1¾-inch muffin tin pressing into the shape of a cup with thumb and fingers. Be careful not to get air pockets under the dough.

FILLING

1   egg
1   tablespoon butter, melted
2   teaspoons vanilla
¾   cup packed light brown sugar
½   cup coarsely chopped nuts

Beat the egg and add butter, vanilla and brown sugar. Mix well. Fill each dough cup about ½ full with this mixture and top with about ⅔ teaspoon nuts. Bake in a preheated 350° oven for 30 minutes or until lightly browned. Filling will puff up. Remove from oven and immediately unmold nut cups from tins with a small knife.

Makes 2 dozen

TOFFEE

2½ cups sugar
½   cup water
¼   cup light corn syrup
2   cups butter
12 ounces semi-sweet or milk chocolate chips
1   cup finely chopped pecans or walnuts

In a medium-size saucepan combine sugar, water, syrup and butter. Cook, stirring constantly until mixture reaches a temperature of 300° on a candy thermometer. Spread candy on a well buttered cookie sheet and sprinkle with chocolate chips. When chips have melted, smooth evenly over candy and sprinkle nuts over all. After toffee has cooled to room temperature, lift off cookie sheet and break into bite-size pieces.

Makes 1½ pounds

PEANUT BRITTLE

2   cups sugar
1   cup light corn syrup
½   cup water
1½ cups raw peanuts
2   tablespoons butter
2   teaspoons vanilla
3½ teaspoons baking soda
½   teaspoon salt

In a large saucepan combine sugar, corn syrup and water. Boil slowly until a candy thermometer reads 230°. Add peanuts and continue boiling until mixture reads 300° on a candy thermometer. Remove from heat and stir in butter, vanilla, soda and salt until well blended. Immediately pour mixture into a well-buttered jelly roll pan and spread out with a spatula. Allow peanut brittle to cool completely and then break into pieces. Store in an air-tight container.

Makes 1 pound

OLD FASHIONED SUCKERS

Fill their "stockings left by the chimney with care" with your homemade suckers. Sucker molds come in a wide range of shapes and sizes, so we will let you determine how many this recipe will make. The molds, as well as a large selection of flavoring oils and food coloring pastes are available at local candy supply shops. For a really red sucker, use the liquid red food coloring as opposed to the paste.

3   cups sugar
1½ cups light corn syrup
1   cup water
1   teaspoon flavoring oil of
    your choice
    food coloring paste of your
    choice

Grease sucker molds with a non-stick spray and secure sticks. Place molds on a marble slab or a greased cookie sheet. In a heavy saucepan combine sugar, corn syrup and water. Cook to 300° on a candy thermometer. Remove from heat and add the flavoring oil and food coloring of your choice. Stir approximately 2 minutes or until well mixed. Pour into sucker molds and allow to set until hardened.

CARAMEL CRUNCH

½ cup packed brown sugar
½ cup light corn syrup
4 tablespoons butter or margarine
½ teaspoon salt
6 cups Chex cereal
1½ cups nuts (unsalted peanuts, walnuts, pecans, almonds, or a mixture of all)

In a 4-quart saucepan heat sugar, syrup, butter and salt until the sugar melts. Stir in the cereal and nuts until coated. Spread the mixture on a cookie sheet and bake in a preheated 250° oven for 30 minutes. Stir occasionally while baking. Remove from oven, cool and store in an air-tight container.

Makes 8 cups

"REECES" CANDY BALLS

On a scale of 1 to 10, our testing team scored these a 12 plus! They are wonderful for holiday gift giving and school bake sales.

½ cup butter, softened
1½ cups creamy peanut butter
3 cups powdered sugar
12 ounces semi-sweet chocolate chips
4 ounces paraffin wax

In a mixing bowl combine butter, peanut butter and powdered sugar. Blend well. Form the dough into 1-inch balls and refrigerate for 20 minutes. In the top of a double boiler over medium heat melt the chocolate chips and paraffin wax. Stir until well blended. Dip the chilled balls into the melted chocolate mixture coating completely. Cool the balls on cookie sheets that have been lined with waxed paper. Refrigerate or store in a cool, dry place.

Makes 5 dozen

Children love to join in the preparations for family gatherings. Encourage them to design individual place cards which can depict the special talents or characteristics of each guest.

FALL IN THE MOUNTAINS

Warm and Spicy Autumn Punch

Southwest Spareribs

Hot Potato Salad

Artichoke Salad

Spicy Carrot Cake

Mount Charleston provides a spectacular view for picnickers. Located in the Spring Mountain Range, Mount Charleston's summit rises to an elevation of nearly 12,000 feet. Picnicking and hiking in the cool, mountain air attracts Las Vegans eager for a change of scenery or temporary respite from the summer heat. During the winter months the area also offers downhill and cross country skiing.

Tableware and accessories provided by Broadway Southwest Department Store

KIFFELS

An old family recipe, these small delicate cookies herald the holiday season.

1   cup butter, softened
6   ounces cream cheese,
    softened
4   egg yolks
2   tablespoons milk
2   cups sifted flour
¼   teaspoon salt

In a mixing bowl cream butter, cheese, egg yolks and milk. Add sifted flour and salt. Mix well. Roll dough into balls about 1-inch in diameter. Refrigerate for at least 6 hours or overnight.

FILLING AND ASSEMBLY

2   egg whites
1   pound walnuts, ground
1¼ cups powdered sugar

Beat egg whites until foamy. Add nuts and ¾ cup of the powdered sugar. With a rolling pin roll out each ball of dough into a 2 to 2½-inch circle. Spread with about 1 teaspoon of the egg white-nut-sugar mixture. Roll up like a cigar and shape into small horseshoes. Place on ungreased cookie sheets and bake in a preheated 350° oven for 35 minutes. Remove from oven and sprinkle with remaining powdered sugar.

Makes 4 to 5 dozen

When using hazelnuts in a recipe you will probably want to remove the skins. To do this, spread whole hazelnuts on a cookie sheet. Bake in a preheated 350° oven 10 to 15 minutes until skins appear loosened. Take nuts from oven and rub between towels to remove skins. Don't be concerned if small portions of skin remain on the nuts. It will not affect the nuts' flavor.

COCONUT TREATS

At Christmas time put each cookie in a tiny holly decorated muffin paper.

2   teaspoons butter or margarine
3   tablespoons water
1   teaspoon vanilla
2   cups sifted powdered sugar
½   cup instant milk powder
3   cups flaked coconut
6   ounces semi-sweet chocolate chips

In a 3-quart saucepan melt butter. Add water and vanilla. Stir well and set aside. Combine powdered sugar and milk powder. Add this mixture, ½ cup at a time, to butter mixture. Blend well. Stir in coconut. Drop by teaspoonfuls onto cookie sheets that have been covered with waxed paper. Refrigerate approximately 15 minutes or until firm. In a small saucepan melt chocolate chips over low heat. Allow to cool slightly and then put a swirl of chocolate on each cookie. Chill ½ hour before storing in an air-tight container.

Makes 3 dozen

CRESCENT COOKIES

For gift giving, line a basket with bright red tissue and pack with an assortment of cookies. Just remember to include our Crescent Cookies.

1½ cups ground almonds
6   tablespoons sugar
2   cups butter or margarine, softened
1   teaspoon vanilla
4   cups flour
    powdered sugar

In a large bowl combine all ingredients except powdered sugar and mix well. For each cookie, shape approximately 1 tablespoon of dough into a crescent on an ungreased cookie sheet. Bake in a preheated 375° oven about 8 to 10 minutes or until lightly browned. When the cookies have cooled, carefully coat them in powdered sugar.

Makes 5 dozen

HAZELNUT COOKIES

Hazelnuts are also called filberts. They are perishable, so we suggest freezing them in an air-tight container until ready to use.

4   egg whites
1   pound powdered sugar
½   pound skinned and ground hazelnuts (see Index)
½   teaspoon grated lemon rind

In a large mixing bowl beat egg whites until stiff. Gradually add sugar, beating constantly and continue to beat for 5 minutes. Into a separate bowl spoon half of the egg white mixture and set aside. To the remaining mixture stir in the nuts and lemon rind. Drop egg-nut mixture by teaspoonfuls onto greased and lightly floured cookie sheets. Take reserved egg white-sugar mixture and swirl on top of the cookies. Allow to dry out for 10 minutes and then bake in a preheated 300° oven 15 minutes or until tops of cookies are delicately brown.

Makes 3 dozen

NO-BAKE CHOCOLATE KISSES

"Deck the halls" with these candy-like cookies that are so quick and easy to make.

1   pound milk chocolate
4   ounces unsweetened baking chocolate
2   cups rice krispies
2   cups pecans, coarsely chopped

In the top of a large double boiler melt the chocolate. When melted, stir in rice krispies and pecans. Remove from heat and drop by teaspoonfuls onto cookie sheets or trays which have been covered with waxed paper. Let sit until hard. You may want to refrigerate the kisses to hasten the hardening process.

Makes 5 dozen

KAHLÚA BALLS

2 cups crushed vanilla wafers (about 48 wafers)
1 cup finely chopped nuts
1 cup powdered sugar
2 tablespoons cocoa
2 tablespoons butter, softened
2 tablespoons dark corn syrup
⅓ cup Kahlúa liqueur

Combine all ingredients in a large bowl. Using your hands, mix well and form into ¾-inch balls. Roll in powdered sugar. Refrigerate in an air-tight container.

Makes 3 dozen

PUMPKIN COOKIES

This is a wonderfully moist cookie.

1 cup vegetable oil
3 cups sugar
2 eggs
5 cups flour
2 teaspoons baking powder
2 teaspoons baking soda
2 teaspoons nutmeg
2 teaspoons cinnamon
1 teaspoon allspice
¼ teaspoon ginger
1¾ teaspoons salt
1 29-ounce can solid pack pumpkin
12 ounces semi-sweet chocolate chips
1 cup chopped walnuts or pecans
3 teaspoons vanilla

In a large mixing bowl blend together the oil and sugar. Add eggs and beat well. Sift together the flour, baking powder, baking soda, nutmeg, cinnamon, allspice, ginger and salt. Add the flour mixture alternately with the pumpkin to the oil-sugar-egg mixture. Beat well after each addition. Fold in chocolate chips, nuts and vanilla. Drop by teaspoonfuls onto greased cookie sheets. Bake in a preheated 350° oven 10 to 12 minutes.

Makes 6 dozen

MORAVIAN PUMPKIN MUFFINS

1⅔ cups sifted flour
¼ teaspoon baking powder
1 teaspoon baking soda
¼ teaspoon salt
1 teaspoon pumpkin pie spice
⅛ teaspoon ground cloves
1½ cups plus 1 tablespoon sugar
⅓ cup butter or margarine, melted
⅓ cup water
2 eggs
1 cup canned pumpkin
⅓ cup raisins

Combine flour, baking powder, baking soda, salt, pumpkin pie spice, cloves and 1½ cups sugar. Set aside. In a mixing bowl blend together the melted butter, water, eggs and pumpkin. To this mixture add the dry ingredients and raisins. Mix just until blended. The batter will seem thick and lumpy. Fill well-greased muffin tins ⅔ full and sprinkle the 1 tablespoon sugar over the muffin tops. Bake in a preheated 400° oven for 20 minutes.

Makes 12

SOUTHERN PECAN PIE

1 9-inch pastry shell, unbaked
1 cup light corn syrup
1 cup packed brown sugar
½ teaspoon salt
⅓ cup butter, melted
1 teaspoon vanilla
3 eggs, beaten
1 cup whole pecans
  whipped cream

In a bowl combine corn syrup, sugar, salt, butter and vanilla. Mix well. Add eggs. Pour into the unbaked pastry shell and sprinkle pecans on top. Bake in a preheated 350° oven for approximately 45 minutes or until set. To serve, you may top with whipped cream.

Serves 6 to 8

NORWEGIAN CHRISTMAS BREAD

2   packages active dry yeast
¾   cup sugar
2   teaspoons salt
½   cup lukewarm water (110°-115°)
1   cup vegetable shortening
1½ cups boiling water
4   eggs, beaten
7-8 cups flour
1½ cups raisins
⅔   cup candied fruit, diced
1   teaspoon ground cardamom

In a small bowl combine yeast, sugar, salt and warm water. Set aside. In a large mixing bowl combine shortening and boiling water. When cool, add eggs and yeast mixture. Add 4 cups of the flour and mix well. Cover and let rise in a warm place until double (about 30 to 60 minutes). Dust raisins and candied fruit with some of the flour. Fold raisins, fruit and ground cardamom into dough. Add enough additional flour to make a stiff but not dry dough. Knead lightly. Divide dough in half and shape into two loaves. Place in greased 9 × 5-inch loaf pans. Let rise until double in bulk. Bake in a preheated 400° oven 10 minutes. Reduce heat to 350° and bake an additional 40 minutes. Remove from oven and turn bread onto racks to cool.

GLAZE

¾   cup powdered sugar
1   teaspoon vanilla
1   tablespoon milk

Combine powdered sugar, vanilla and milk. Mix until smooth. Drizzle glaze over loaves.

Makes 2 loaves

Dated Christmas ornaments make perfect holiday table favors—from year to year they will remind us of good times shared with good friends.

CRANBERRY MUFFINS

When cranberries are in season buy several extra bags and freeze. You will then be able to enjoy this delicious muffin throughout the year.

1   cup fresh cranberries, coarsely chopped
¾ cup sugar
1   egg, beaten
1   cup buttermilk
4   tablespoons butter or margarine, melted
2   cups flour
¾ teaspoon baking soda
¼ teaspoon salt

Toss the cranberries with ½ cup of the sugar. Set aside. Combine egg, buttermilk and butter in a bowl. Mix well. Sift together flour, baking soda, salt and the remaining ¼ cup sugar in a large bowl. Make a well in the dry ingredients and add milk mixture all at once. Stir until moistened. Gently fold in cranberries. Fill greased muffin tins ⅔ full. Bake in a preheated 400° oven for 20 minutes. Serve hot.

Makes 12

PUMPKIN NUT BREAD

3½ cups flour
2   teaspoons baking soda
1   teaspoon salt
1   teaspoon cinnamon
1   teaspoon nutmeg
3   cups sugar
4   eggs, beaten
1   cup chopped pecans
1½ cups canned pumpkin
1   cup vegetable oil
⅔ cup water

Sift flour, baking soda, salt, cinnamon, nutmeg and sugar into a large mixing bowl. Add eggs, pecans, pumpkin, oil and water to dry ingredients. Mix only until dry ingredients are moistened. Pour into two well-greased loaf pans. Bake in a preheated 350° oven 1 hour or until a toothpick inserted in the center comes out clean. Cool on wire rack.

TOPPING

2   tablespoons butter, melted
2   tablespoons sugar
½ teaspoon cinnamon

Brush warm bread with melted butter. Combine sugar and cinnamon and sprinkle over bread.

Makes 2 loaves

PECAN CRANBERRY CAKE

5   cups flour
2   cups sugar
1   teaspoon salt
2   teaspoons baking powder
2   teaspoons baking soda
4   eggs, beaten
2   cups buttermilk
1½ cups vegetable oil
2   cups chopped pecans
2   cups chopped dates
    grated rind of 4 oranges
2   cups fresh whole cranberries

GLAZE

2   cups fresh orange juice
2   cups sugar
4   tablespoons Grand Marnier
    liqueur

In a large mixing bowl sift together 4 cups of the flour, sugar, salt, baking powder and baking soda. Add eggs, buttermilk and oil and beat well. Roll pecans, dates and orange rinds in remaining cup of flour and fold into the cake mixture. Gently blend in cranberries. Pour batter into a greased bundt pan. Bake cake in a preheated 350° oven for 10 minutes. Reduce heat to 300° and continue to bake for 60 to 75 minutes or until cake tests done. Remove cake from pan and cool on wire rack.

While cake is cooling combine juice, sugar and Grand Marnier. Mix well. Place a drip pan under cooled cake and slowly drizzle glaze over cake until all is absorbed. Refrigerate at least 2 hours before serving.

Serves 10 to 12

A convenient way to keep buttermilk on hand for baking is to maintain a supply in your freezer. Using storage containers, freeze in quantities most appropriate for your cooking needs. For best results do not store longer than 3 weeks.

GRANDMA'S PUMPKIN CAKE

4 eggs
2 cups sugar (or 1 cup honey)
⅔ cup vegetable oil
2 cups flour
2 teaspoons baking soda
1 teaspoon salt
2 cups pumpkin
1 teaspoon cinnamon
½ teaspoon nutmeg
½ teaspoon ground cloves

In a large mixing bowl beat together the eggs, sugar and oil. Sift together remaining ingredients. Gradually add to the egg mixture and beat 2 minutes. Pour the batter into 2 greased and lightly floured 9-inch round cake pans or one 9 × 13-inch pan. Bake in a preheated 325° oven for 40 to 50 minutes or until a toothpick inserted in the center comes out clean. Cool for 20 minutes. Turn cakes out on a rack and cool completely.

FROSTING

½ cup butter or margarine
8 ounces cream cheese, softened
1 teaspoon vanilla
1 pound powdered sugar
½ cup chopped walnuts or pecans (optional)

In a large mixing bowl beat butter and cream cheese together until fluffy. Blend in the vanilla and powdered sugar. Stir in the nuts and frost cooled cake.

Serves 12

FROZEN CRANBERRY VELVET PIE

Our Frozen Cranberry Velvet Pie makes a festive finale to your holiday entertaining.

6 tablespoons butter or margarine
1¼ cups finely crushed vanilla wafers (30 wafers)
1 cup heavy cream
¼ cup sugar
½ teaspoon vanilla
8 ounces cream cheese, softened
1 16-ounce can whole cranberry sauce

In a saucepan melt butter. Add crushed wafers and mix well. Press into bottom and up sides of a buttered 9-inch pie plate. Chill while preparing the filling. In a small mixing bowl combine cream, sugar and vanilla. Whip until thickened but not stiff. In a separate mixing bowl beat cream cheese until fluffy. Gradually add whipped cream mixture to cream cheese, beating until smooth. Set aside ¼ cup cranberry sauce for garnish. Fold the remaining cranberry sauce into the whipped mixture. Spoon into the chilled crust and freeze until firm. Remove from freezer 20 to 25 minutes before serving. To serve, top each slice with reserved cranberry sauce.

Serves 8 to 12

HOLIDAY FRUIT CAKE

Package with a bow and treat your holiday hosts and friends to this flavorful and traditional cake. Don't forget to include the recipe.

1   pound pitted dates
4   cups pecan halves
6   ounces whole candied red cherries
6   ounces whole candied green cherries
6   ounces candied pineapple
4   eggs
1   cup sugar
1   cup flour
1   teaspoon baking powder
½   teaspoon salt

Line three 3⅝ × 7⅜-inch loaf pans with brown paper. To do this cut 2 strips for each pan from a brown paper sack. One should fit the width of the pan and the other the length. Overlap them in the pan with ends extending above the pan rim. Set aside. In a large bowl combine dates, pecans and candied fruits. Stir to mix thoroughly. If fruits stick together sprinkle with a little of the flour. Set aside. In a separate bowl beat eggs. Add sugar and continue to beat until well mixed, but not foamy. Sift flour, baking powder and salt into egg mixture and blend well. Pour batter over fruits and nuts, making sure that they are well coated with batter. Divide batter-covered fruit evenly among the 3 lined pans. Bake in a preheated 300° oven 1¼ hours. The loaves should be golden brown and somewhat firm. While piping hot turn cakes out onto racks and remove brown paper. When cool, wrap in foil and refrigerate. To serve, slice very thin.

Makes 3 loaves

Pomegranates, like cranberries, have a short harvest season and limited shelf life. To enjoy their flavor year round, crack and seed pomegranates at season's peak. Freeze seeds in an air-tight container for later use. Sprinkle in fresh green salads for a delightful change of color and texture.

SWEET POTATO AUTUMN

4 cups finely grated sweet
  potatoes
2 cups milk
2 cups dark brown sugar
1 cup raisins
4 tablespoons butter or
  margarine, melted
1 teaspoon salt
½ teaspoon cinnamon
½ teaspoon allspice
½ teaspoon ginger
½ teaspoon ground cloves
4 eggs, slightly beaten

In a large mixing bowl combine all ingredients, stirring well. Place in a greased 2-quart casserole and bake in a preheated 350° oven for 30 minutes. Stir mixture and bake an additional hour.

Serves 6

CHESTNUT AND SAUSAGE STUFFING

Most of us have a time-honored family recipe for stuffing turkey, but we think that once you have tried our chestnut-sausage combination you might just have an additional favorite.

1 one-pound loaf unsliced day-
  old white bread
½ tablespoon salt
1 teaspoon pepper
1 teaspoon thyme
1 teaspoon oregano
1 cup butter
1¼ cups minced onions
1 pound pork sausage
½ pound cooked ham, chopped
½ cup minced celery
¼ cup minced parsley
3 eggs, beaten
½ cup half and half
1 pound braised chestnuts
  (1 15½-ounce can whole
  chestnuts in water, drained
  and chopped, may be
  substituted)

Remove crusts from bread and discard. Cut loaf into small cubes. Toast cubes in a preheated 325° oven until lightly brown. Put cubes in a large bowl and add salt, pepper, thyme and oregano. Toss well. In a large skillet melt butter and sauté onions until soft. Add sausage to skillet and crumble. Continue cooking until meat is browned. Add ham, celery and parsley to the sausage and mix well. Remove from heat and add mixture to bread cubes. Add beaten eggs and half and half. Mix well. Fold chopped chestnuts into the stuffing mixture. Extra stuffing may be cooked in a greased casserole along with the turkey for about 45 minutes. Refrigerate if made ahead.

Makes 10 cups

Southwestern Fare

TRADITIONAL SANGRÍA

If you have a ceramic crock, use it for offering this hospitable drink. The thickness of the crock insulates the Sangría. When ladling into glasses be sure to include a portion of the fruit.

3   lemons
3   oranges
4   cups dry red wine
1   cup brandy
1   quart club soda
¾   cup sugar
2   trays ice cubes
    assorted fruits (pineapple chunks, apple cubes, halved cherries, etc.)

Squeeze the juice from the lemons and the oranges. Reserve the rinds from 1 lemon and 1 orange and cut into strips. In a large pitcher combine the juices, red wine, brandy, club soda, sugar and ice cubes. Stir. Add the rinds and whatever other fruits you have selected.

Makes 2½ quarts

FRESH SANGRÍA BLANCO

The sweetness of Sangría lends balance to the spicy flavors of Southwestern dishes. This white wine Sangría is particularly refreshing on a warm summer day.

½   cup sugar
½   cup fresh lemon juice
½   cup fresh orange juice
¼   cup Curaçao or Grand Marnier liqueur
3½ cups dry white wine
1   10-ounce bottle club soda, chilled
    orange slices
    lemon slices

In a 3-quart container dissolve sugar in lemon juice and orange juice. Add liqueur and wine. Chill. When ready to serve add the club soda. Garnish with orange and lemon slices.

Serves 4

MARGARITAS

Say "mi casa es su casa" with our frothy margaritas.

1   lime
    margarita salt
6   ounces sweet-and-sour bar
    mix
4   ounces tequila
2½ ounces Triple Sec liqueur
1½ teaspoons sugar
    ice

Cut lime into quarters. For each glass: rub a lime quarter around rim, dip rim into salt, and squeeze the juice from the lime quarter into the glass. In a blender combine sweet-and-sour mix, tequila, Triple Sec and sugar. Fill container with ice. Blend on medium speed and then on high until ice is finely crushed. Pour into margarita glasses and serve.

Serves 4

GUACAMOLE

Bravo to the avocado!!

2   ripe avocados
2   tablespoons finely chopped
    onion
1   large tomato, peeled, seeded
    and chopped
1   garlic clove, minced
1   4-ounce can diced green
    chiles
1½ teaspoons lemon juice
    salt
    pepper

Cut avocados in half, peel and pit. In a bowl mash avocados coarsely and add onion, tomato, garlic, chiles and lemon juice. Mix well. Season with salt and pepper. Accompany with a large bowl of tortilla chips.

Makes 1½ to 2 cups

SUNSET SALSA FRIA

These two fresh salsas can be used as an accompaniment to any of our Southwestern recipes or as a dip for tortilla chips.

2	pounds ripe tomatoes, chopped
½	cup peeled, seeded and chopped fresh California green chiles (see Index)
1	large sweet onion, chopped
1	garlic clove, minced
½	teaspoon minced cilantro
	salt
2	tablespoons lemon juice

In a bowl combine the tomatoes, chiles and onion. Mix well. Add garlic, salt, cilantro and lemon juice. Mix again and chill.

Makes 3 cups

SPICY SALSA SUPREMA

For a milder salsa, reduce the amount of minced jalapeño pepper.

2	28-ounce cans tomatoes, drained and chopped
4	green onions (tops included), chopped
¼	cup chopped fresh cilantro
1	jalapeño pepper, seeded and minced
4	fresh California green chiles, peeled, seeded and chopped (see Index)
	juice of 1 lemon
	juice of 1 lime
1	teaspoon salt

Combine all ingredients in a large bowl and mix well. Refrigerate until ready to use. Flavors are enhanced if made one day before serving.

Makes 2 quarts

FIESTA SURPRISE DIP

1   16-ounce can refried beans
3   ripe avocados, peeled and
    pitted
2   tablespoons lemon juice
    salt
    pepper
    garlic powder
1   cup sour cream
½   package dry taco seasoning
3   tablespoons mayonnaise
½   cup shredded Monterey Jack
    cheese
½   cup shredded Cheddar cheese
2   tomatoes, chopped
½   cup chopped green onions
½   cup sliced black olives
    tortilla or corn chips

Spread beans in a shallow (1½-inch deep) pie plate or round serving dish with sides. Mash avocados and combine with lemon juice, salt, pepper and garlic powder to taste. Spread over beans. Combine sour cream, taco seasoning and mayonnaise. Spread over avocados. Layer remaining ingredients in the following order: Monterey Jack cheese, Cheddar cheese, tomatoes, green onions, and olives. Serve with a basket of tortilla chips.

Serves 10

CHAFING DISH BEEF AND BEANS

1   pound ground beef
¼   cup chopped onion
¼   teaspoon garlic powder
2   7-ounce cans green chile salsa
1   16-ounce can spicy refried
    beans
1   teaspoon salt
½   cup grated Cheddar cheese

In a skillet brown beef and crumble. Drain off excess grease. Add onion and garlic powder and cook until onion is soft. Add salsa, refried beans and salt. Continue cooking until mixture is hot and bubbly. Spoon into a chafing dish and top with cheese. Serve with warmed tortilla chips.

Serves 8 to 10

LA BANDERA DE MEXICO PARTY DIP

½ pound ground beef
½ pound Mexican chorizo sausage (hot Italian sausage may be substituted)
1 medium onion, diced
   salt
1 cup grated Cheddar cheese
1 cup Monterey Jack cheese
2 16-ounce cans refried beans
1 4-ounce can diced green chiles
½ cup taco sauce
¾ cup chopped green onions
1 cup diced black olives
2 cups guacamole (see Index)
1 cup sour cream
2 canned long pimientos

In a large skillet brown meats and onion. Drain off grease and salt meat to taste. Set aside. In a bowl combine cheeses and toss to mix. In a large 2 to 3-inch deep casserole layer ingredients in the following order: refried beans, meat and onion mixture, chiles, mixed cheeses and taco sauce. Bake, uncovered, in a preheated 400° oven for 20 minutes. Remove casserole from oven and sprinkle evenly with green onions and olives. Mound the guacamole in the center of the casserole. Top the guacamole with sour cream. Make a cross with the whole pimientos on top of the sour cream and serve with an abundance of tortilla chips.

Serves 12

To peel chiles preheat oven broiler and raise oven rack to the highest position. Turning often, broil chiles until brown and blistered on all sides, about 15 minutes. As each chile is done immediately seal in a plastic bag until cool enough to handle, about 5 to 10 minutes. The steam contained in the bag helps to loosen the skin. Remove the skin with a paring knife and discard.

TACO SALAD

This hearty main course salad makes a great Sunday supper. Serve with spicy salsa and extra shredded cheese on the table.

1	pound ground beef
1	package dry taco seasoning
1	16-ounce can red kidney beans (optional)
1	large head iceberg lettuce, shredded
1	red onion, chopped
4	large tomatoes, diced
2	large avocados, peeled, pitted and diced
1	cup grated Cheddar cheese
1	8-ounce package tortilla chips, crushed

In a large skillet sauté meat until brown and crumbled. Drain off excess grease. Sprinkle with taco seasoning and mix well. Stir in kidney beans and allow mixture to cool. In a very large bowl combine lettuce, onion, tomatoes, avocados, cheese and tortilla chips. Add meat mixture. Set aside while preparing dressing.

DRESSING

2	cups sour cream
1	teaspoon salt
2	tablespoons mayonnaise
1	teaspoon picante sauce pepper

In a bowl combine sour cream, salt, mayonnaise, picante sauce and pepper to taste. Stir well and pour over salad. Toss thoroughly and serve immediately.

Serves 6 to 8

To soften and warm flour tortillas, we recommend the following method. Wrap 6 tortillas in a tea towel or large linen napkin. Place in a colander or steamer over simmering water for approximately 5 minutes. Transfer, still covered, to a basket and serve immediately. If preparing burros, burritos, or a similar dish, use tortillas while still pliable.

HERMOSILLO CHEESE SOUP

The contributor of this recipe created it after savoring the "original" in a little restaurant in picturesque Hermosillo, the capital city of the Northern Mexican State of Sonora.

4   large russet potatoes, peeled and cubed
2½ quarts water
1   teaspoon salt
3   chicken flavored bouillon cubes
1   7-ounce can whole green chiles, cut into ¼ × 2-inch strips
1   4-ounce jar sliced pimientos
6   large celery stalks, diced
1   medium onion, diced
¾   pound Monterey Jack cheese, shredded
¾   pound Monterey Jack cheese, thinly sliced
    Tabasco sauce

Place cubed potatoes in a pot of rapidly boiling water. When water returns to a boil cook for 5 minutes. Drain potatoes and rinse with hot tap water. Set aside. In a 4-quart saucepan combine the 2½ quarts water, salt and bouillon cubes. Bring liquid to a boil over high heat and add rinsed potatoes, chiles, pimientos, celery and onion. Cover and simmer 20 minutes. Divide shredded cheese equally among 8 soup bowls. Ladle hot soup over the shredded cheese. Place 2 to 3 slices of cheese on top of each bowl and serve immediately with warm buttered tortillas. Offer Tabasco sauce for those who like HOT soup!

Serves 8

SOUTH OF THE BORDER SOUP

This recipe is our version of the traditional tortilla soup!

1   large onion, diced
1   large green pepper, diced
1   large tomato, diced
2   tablespoons minced parsley
2   8-ounce cans tomato sauce
3¾ cups chicken broth
¼   teaspoon thyme
½   teaspoon salt
    fresh black pepper
    dash of Tabasco
    tortilla chips
2   cups grated Monterey Jack cheese

In a Dutch oven combine onion, green pepper, tomato, parsley, tomato sauce, chicken broth and seasonings. Simmer for 20 minutes. In each of four individual soup bowls place a handful of tortilla chips and ½ cup of the grated cheese. Ladle soup into bowls over the chips and cheese.

Serves 4

ALBONDIGAS SOUP

Serve this Mexican soup with warmed flour tortillas.

MEATBALLS

1	pound ground beef
1	cup dry bread crumbs
1	egg, beaten
¾	teaspoon chili powder
	salt to taste

Combine all ingredients for meatballs and mix well. Roll into balls about 1-inch in diameter. Set aside.

SOUP BASE

8	cups beef broth
1	16-ounce can stewed tomatoes
1	cup peeled and chopped carrots
1	cup chopped celery
1	medium onion, chopped
4	tablespoons canned diced chiles
1	tablespoon salsa
	salt to taste
	pepper to taste
1	garlic clove, minced
1	tablespoon minced parsley
1	cup cooked white rice

In a 5-quart Dutch oven combine all ingredients except rice. Bring to a slow rolling boil. Drop meatballs into the boiling broth one at a time. Cook soup for 30 minutes stirring gently. Add rice and simmer an additional 10 minutes.

Serves 6 to 8

Complete your fiesta with this flavorful coffee. To each cup of coffee add a touch of Kahlúa. Top with whipped cream and dot with a whole coffee bean. Serve immediately using cinnamon sticks as stirrers.

CASSEROLE OLÉ

3   medium zucchini, thinly sliced
2   cups cooked white rice
1   7-ounce can diced green chiles
¾   pound Monterey Jack cheese, grated
1   large tomato, thinly sliced
     salt
2   cups sour cream
1   teaspoon oregano
1   teaspoon garlic salt
¼   cup chopped green onion
¼   cup chopped green pepper
2   tablespoons minced parsley

In a saucepan cook zucchini in a small amount of salted water until tender but crisp. Place the rice in a buttered 3-quart ovenproof casserole. Cover with chiles and sprinkle with half of the cheese. Arrange zucchini and tomato slices on top and sprinkle with salt. In a separate bowl combine sour cream, oregano, garlic salt, onion and green pepper. Spoon this mixture over the tomato-zucchini layer and sprinkle the remaining cheese over all. Bake in a preheated 350° oven 30 to 35 minutes or until heated through. Just before serving garnish with parsley.

Serves 8

MEXICAN OMELET

1   ripe avocado, peeled, pitted and mashed
¼   cup sour cream
2   tablespoons canned diced green chiles
1   tablespoon chopped green onion
1   teaspoon lemon juice
¼   teaspoon salt
     dash of Tabasco
2   tablespoons butter
1   corn tortilla, torn in bite-size pieces
6   eggs, beaten
1   cup shredded Monterey Jack cheese
     salsa

Combine avocado, sour cream, chiles, green onion, lemon juice, salt and Tabasco. Set aside. Melt butter in a 10-inch ovenproof skillet. Add tortilla pieces and cook until soft. Pour in beaten eggs and cook 3 to 5 minutes. Lift the edges of the eggs to allow uncooked portion to flow under. Remove from heat and sprinkle cheese over the top. Place skillet in a preheated 325° oven and bake 3 to 4 minutes or until cheese melts. Remove from oven and spread avocado mixture on top. Return to oven and bake an additional 5 to 7 minutes. Fold in half and serve on a warmed platter. Top with salsa.

Serves 6

HUEVOS RANCHEROS FOR A CROWD

This recipe may also be prepared in individual ramekins. Pour equal amounts of sauce into ramekins. Instead of beating the eggs merely crack 1 or 2 over the sauce in each ramekin and puncture yolks with a fork. Top with cheese and green onions and bake in a preheated 300° oven for 20 minutes. To make your fiesta complete serve with Chile Con Queso, steamed tortillas and butter, a fresh fruit platter, our Mexican Swizzle Sticks and Margaritas.

4	tablespoons butter or margarine
1	cup flour
6	7-ounce cans green chile salsa
1¾	cups water
2	2¼-ounce cans chopped or sliced black olives
1	cup chopped green onions
4	cups grated Cheddar cheese
32	eggs, slightly beaten

In a 5-quart Dutch oven melt butter over medium heat. Gradually add flour, whisking constantly to make a roux. Stir in chile salsa and water blending well. Add olives, ½ cup of the green onions and 2 cups cheese. Continue stirring until cheese has melted. Pour sauce equally into two 11 × 13-inch ovenproof casseroles. Over this pour the slightly beaten eggs, again dividing equally between the 2 casseroles. Sprinkle the casseroles with the remaining 2 cups of shredded cheese and remaining ½ cup onions. Bake in a preheated 300° oven for 50 to 60 minutes.

Serves 20 to 24

Fresh hot chile peppers can add spice to your Southwestern fare; however, care must be taken in handling them during preparation. The released oils of a chopped hot chile can severely burn the skin and eyes for several hours. The best way to avoid this is to wear rubber gloves.

BEEF BURROS

Burros are a popular Southwestern sandwich. If you are not feeding a crowd, freeze remaining meat filling for use at a later date.

4   pounds beef stew meat
1   4-ounce can diced green chiles
    water
¼   cup chopped onions
1   garlic clove, minced
2   tablespoons vegetable oil
2½ cups chicken broth
1   tablespoon chili powder
¼   cup flour
1   teaspoon salt
1¼ cups red chile sauce (enchilada sauce may be substituted)
8-10 12-inch flour tortillas, softened (see Index)
    shredded cheese
    chopped green onions

Place stew meat and green chiles in a Dutch oven. Add water to cover and simmer 2 to 3 hours. In a medium-size skillet sauté onions and garlic in oil until lightly brown. Add chicken broth and bring mixture to a simmer. Blend in chili powder, flour, salt and chile sauce. Simmer 30 minutes. Add broth mixture to meat during the last hour meat is cooking. Simmer 1 hour, stirring occasionally. Shred meat with fork. To assemble burros divide meat mixture among 8 to 10 flour tortillas. Lap ends of tortilla over meat and then fold sides to center to enclose filling. Serve seam side down. Garnish with shredded cheese and chopped green onions. Accompany with refried beans.

Serves 8 to 10

FISH MEXICANO

Individual servings of our Fish Mexicano may be served over a warmed tortilla or steamed white rice.

2   tablespoons vegetable oil
2   large tomatoes, diced
1   medium onion, diced
1   teaspoon minced cilantro
1½ cups green chile salsa
1½ pounds red snapper fillets
4   slices Monterey Jack cheese
4   slices Cheddar cheese
4   slices avocado

In a large skillet heat oil and sauté tomatoes and onion. Stir in cilantro and chile salsa. Place fish fillets over this mixture and cook approximately 5 minutes. Turn fish over and cook until almost done. Arrange cheese slices over each serving and continue to cook until cheese has melted. Garnish each fillet of fish with sliced avocado and serve.

Serves 4

FIESTA PARA DOS

Traditional Sangría

Guacamole

Spicy Salsa

Tortilla Chips

Chile Con Queso

Beef Cilantro

Mexican Swizzle Sticks

Just 20 miles west of downtown Las Vegas, Red Rock Canyon offers dramatic scenery for picnickers and explorers alike. Its terra cotta mountains are the perfect backdrop for our picnic of Southwestern fare. The Red Rock Canyon Visitor Center and Scenic Loop Drive provide fascinating information about attractions in the area which include fossil beds, petroglyphs and wildlife.

Picnic furnishings provided by Goldwaters Department Store

BEEF CILANTRO

Cilantro is the fresh leaves of the coriander plant. Similar to parsley in appearance, its flavor is unique. It is a very popular ingredient in Mexican dishes. If time is a factor, substitute warmed flour tortillas or pita bread for the homemade tortilla crepes. Our Beef Cilantro is also excellent as a taco filling.

1	cup cooked pinto beans, drained (reserve liquid)
2	tablespoons vegetable oil
1	pound beef-stew meat, cut into bite-size pieces
1	medium onion, diced
2	tomatoes, diced
⅓	cup chopped fresh cilantro
1	teaspoon chili powder
1½	teaspoons ground cumin
	salt
	pepper
	tortilla crepes

If necessary add enough water to the bean liquid to make 1½ cups. Set aside. Heat oil in a large skillet and brown the beef. Reduce heat and add the reserved bean liquid. Cover and simmer 1 hour or until the beef is tender. Stir in onion, tomatoes, cilantro, chili powder, cumin and reserved beans. Season to taste with salt and pepper. Cook uncovered over medium heat for 15 minutes or until sauce is thick. Stir occasionally. Fill warm tortilla crepes with beef mixture and roll up to serve.

TORTILLA CREPES

Masa Harina is a dehydrated corn flour. Look for it near the similarly packaged all-purpose flour at your grocery store.

3	eggs
1¼	cups milk
2	tablespoons vegetable oil
½	cup Masa Harina
½	cup flour
½	teaspoon salt

Beat eggs with milk and oil. Gradually add remaining ingredients. Let stand one hour. Preheat an omelet or sauté pan and brush lightly with oil. Use ¼ cup batter for each crepe and over medium-high heat fry quickly on both sides.

Serves 4

CHICKEN CHILE EMPANADAS

Go ahead and assemble these main course Mexican turnovers early in the day. Just be sure to cover them tightly with plastic wrap and refrigerate until ready to deep fry.

FILLING

2	cups shredded cooked chicken or turkey
1	7-ounce can diced green chiles
¼	cup sour cream

Combine all ingredients in a small bowl and mix well. Cover and refrigerate.

DOUGH

4	cups Masa Harina
5	teaspoons baking powder
¼	cup grated Cheddar cheese
2¾	cups warm chicken broth
	oil for deep frying

In a large bowl combine Masa Harina, baking powder and cheese. Mix well. Add chicken broth and stir until dough is smooth. Cover and let rest 5 minutes. Shape dough into balls about the size of walnuts and cover with a damp cloth. Pat each ball between the palms of your hands into a circle about 3-inches in diameter. Place 1 rounded teaspoon of filling in the center of the dough and fold sides together to make a half moon. Seal edges firmly with fingers or fork. Cover with a damp cloth until you complete the remaining empanadas. When ready to cook heat oil in a deep fat fryer to 375°. In batches, deep fry empanadas until golden brown. Drain well and keep warm. Serve with a spicy salsa.

Makes 3½ dozen

CHILE RELLENO CASSEROLE

1	4-ounce can whole green chiles
½	pound Cheddar cheese, grated
¼	pound Monterey Jack cheese, grated
1	onion, chopped
3	eggs
⅓	cup flour
⅛	teaspoon salt
2	cups milk
½	cup ketchup
6	ounces mozzarella cheese, grated
¾	cup salsa

Grease a 1½-quart shallow casserole. Remove seeds from chiles, cut into 1-inch wide strips and arrange in bottom of casserole. Cover with Cheddar and Monterey Jack cheeses and onion. In a separate bowl beat eggs lightly, adding flour and salt. Slowly add milk. Pour egg-milk mixture over cheeses. Bake in a preheated 325° oven for 50 minutes. Remove casserole from oven and spread with ketchup. Sprinkle with mozzarella cheese and top with salsa. Return casserole to oven and bake an additional 5 to 10 minutes or until cheese is melted.

Serves 8

CHILE CON QUESO

3	tablespoons butter or margarine
2	medium green peppers, diced
1	medium onion, minced
1	16-ounce can tomatoes
1	teaspoon chili powder
¼	teaspoon salt
2	cups grated sharp Cheddar cheese

In a skillet melt butter and sauté green peppers and onion until tender. Add tomatoes, chili powder and salt. Stir well, breaking tomatoes apart with a fork. Simmer 10 minutes. Add cheese and allow to melt over low heat. Do not allow to boil. Serve warm in a chafing dish or fondue pot with tortilla chips. Stir several times while serving to maintain smoothness of cheese.

Serves 6

NEVADA GREEN CHILE STRATA

12 slices bread, trimmed, buttered and cut into small cubes
1 pound Cheddar cheese, shredded
1 pound bacon, cooked and crumbled
  chopped parsley
1 4-ounce can diced green chiles
6 eggs, beaten
4 cups milk
1½ teaspoons minced onion
¼ teaspoon salt
  pepper
½ teaspoon dry mustard

Place cubed bread in a 9 × 13-inch greased ovenproof dish. Sprinkle with ¾ of the cheese. Add bacon, parsley and green chiles. In a bowl combine eggs, milk, onion, salt, pepper and dry mustard. Mix well and pour over other ingredients. Mix lightly with a fork and sprinkle the remaining cheese on top. *Refrigerate overnight.* Bake uncovered in a preheated 350° oven for 45 minutes.

Serves 12

CORN AND GREEN CHILE CASSEROLE

2 cups frozen corn
2 large eggs, beaten
½ cup yellow cornmeal
1 4-ounce can diced green chiles
1 teaspoon salt
½ cup butter or margarine, melted
1 cup sour cream
½ pound Monterey Jack cheese, cubed

Combine all ingredients and mix well. Place in a greased 1½-quart casserole and bake in a preheated 350° oven for 1 hour.

Serves 4 to 6

CHAYOTE

Also known as pear squash, the increasingly popular chayote is native to the cool highlands of Central America, and boasts a low caloric content. Before peeling this vegetable, protect your hands by rubbing them lightly with vegetable oil. Afterward, rub with lime peels and wash in warm soapy water.

2	pounds chayote
4	tablespoons butter or margarine, melted
	juice of 1 lime
1	teaspoon sugar
½	teaspoon salt
¼	teaspoon Tabasco
2	tablespoons chopped cilantro

Peel chayote and cut into 1-inch cubes including edible seeds. Place in a 3-quart saucepan and cover with boiling water. Boil chayote until fork tender. Combine all remaining ingredients in a small bowl and whisk well. Drain chayote and toss with whisked dressing. Serve hot.

Serves 6

PICKLED JICAMA

A Mexican root vegetable, the jicama is similar to the potato in texture but has a sweeter flavor.

1	medium jicama, peeled and thinly sliced
½	cup water
½	cup vinegar
1	medium onion, sliced
4	garlic cloves, peeled
1	teaspoon sugar
	salt
⅓	cup vegetable oil
1	teaspoon pepper
1	teaspoon oregano
1	bay leaf

Place jicama in a saucepan. Add water, vinegar, onion, garlic, sugar and salt. Bring mixture to a boil and simmer until jicama is tender. Add oil, pepper, oregano and bay leaf. Continue to boil for 5 minutes. Remove from heat and cool to room temperature. Refrigerate at least 24 hours before serving.

Makes 3½ cups

SOUTHWEST CORNBREAD

1 cup yellow cornmeal
½ teaspoon salt
½ teaspoon baking soda
⅔ cup buttermilk
2 eggs, beaten
1 17-ounce can creamed corn
⅓ cup butter or margarine, melted
1 cup grated sharp Cheddar cheese
1 4-ounce can diced green chiles

Grease a 9-inch square baking dish. In a bowl combine cornmeal, salt, baking soda, buttermilk, eggs, corn and butter. Mix well. Pour half of the batter into the baking dish and sprinkle with all of the cheese and chiles. Cover with the remaining batter. Bake in a preheated 375° oven for 40 minutes or until golden brown. Cut into squares to serve.

Serves 4 to 6

ALMOND FLAN

Flan is baked in a warm-water bath to maintain an even cooking temperature throughout the custard.

1¼ cups sugar
3 tablespoons water
⅓ cup blanched almonds
2 cups milk
¼ teaspoon salt
1 cinnamon stick
2 whole eggs
3 egg yolks

In a heavy skillet cook ¾ cup of the sugar and water over moderate heat until it has melted and turned pale golden in color. Coat the bottom and sides of a flan pan or a 9 or 10-inch glass pie plate with this carmelized sugar. Set aside. In a food processor or blender combine almonds with a little of the milk. Process until almonds are finely ground. Combine almonds, remaining milk, remaining sugar, salt and cinnamon in a saucepan. Bring mixture to a boil and then reduce heat. Simmer for 20 minutes stirring occasionally. Let cool slightly. Remove cinnamon stick. In a mixing bowl beat whole eggs and egg yolks together. Gradually beat in the warm milk mixture. Pour into the carmel-coated pan which has been placed in a larger pan containing approximately ½-inch of hot water. Bake in a preheated 325° oven 45 to 60 minutes or until a knife inserted in the flan comes out clean. Cool to room temperature and then refrigerate for at least 2 hours before turning out onto a large platter.

Serves 6 to 8

DEEP FRIED ICE CREAM

Ingredients in this recipe are easily increased or decreased depending upon the number of servings.

3 cups sugarless corn flakes, slightly crushed
½ gallon ice cream
4 teaspoons ground cinnamon
oil for deep frying
honey
whipped cream
8 maraschino cherries

Place corn flakes in a medium-size bowl. One at a time shape the ice cream into 8 balls, sprinkling each ball with cinnamon and then rolling in the crushed corn flakes. Place on a cookie sheet and freeze until very hard. (You might want to reduce your freezer to a colder temperature.) Chill serving dishes. Just before serving fill a deep fat fryer with enough oil to totally submerge the ice cream balls and heat oil to a temperature of 375°. One at a time deep fry ice cream balls for 3 to 5 seconds. Place in a chilled serving dish and top with honey, whipped cream and a cherry.

Serves 8

MEXICAN SWIZZLE STICKS

½ cup butter or margarine
¾ cup powdered sugar
1 egg
1 teaspoon vanilla
½ teaspoon cinnamon
1¼ cups flour
1 ounce unsweetened chocolate, melted

In a large mixing bowl combine butter, sugar, egg, vanilla and cinnamon. Mix well. Slowly blend in flour and add melted chocolate. Stir until smooth. Fill a pastry bag with batter and using the star "tip" make 4-inch strips on an ungreased cookie sheet. Bake 5 to 7 minutes in a preheated 375° oven. Cool.

CHOCOLATE GLAZE

1 cup powdered sugar
1 ounce unsweetened chocolate, melted
4 tablespoons milk

To prepare chocolate glaze combine powdered sugar, melted chocolate and milk. Drizzle over the swizzle sticks.

Makes 4 dozen

Dining on the Town

BOUILLABAISSE *(Frontier Hotel)*

The chef noted that you can vary the amounts and types of fish and shellfish depending upon their availability. A green salad and French bread completes the menu for this satisfying meal as featured in Diamond Jim's.

½   cup olive oil
1   pound fish bones
2½ quarts water
2   cups dry white wine
2   teaspoons salt
2   sprigs fresh thyme
4   sprigs fresh parsley
2   leeks, diced (reserve green stems for stock)
1   small onion, diced (reserve trimmings for stock)
2   fish flavored bouillon cubes
10   medium shrimp, shelled (rub shells with two split garlic cloves and reserve for stock)
1½ pounds lobster
3½ pounds firm fish (halibut, bass, turbot, red snapper or a similar fish) cut into bite-size pieces
10   small Little Neck clams in shell
1   teaspoon saffron
1   teaspoon finely ground pepper
6   medium tomatoes, peeled and diced
½   cup minced parsley

In a 6 to 8-quart stockpot heat oil over moderate heat. Add fish bones and sauté lightly for 3 minutes. Add water, wine, salt, thyme, parsley, leek greens, onion trimmings and shrimp shells. Bring to a boil. Reduce heat and simmer 20 minutes. Strain the stock through a fine sieve or several layers of cheese cloth. If stock needs more flavoring, add the fish flavored bouillon cubes. Bring stock back to a boil and add shrimp, lobster, fish, clams, saffron, pepper, leeks and onions. After 8 minutes add tomatoes and minced parsley. Cook 4 minutes.

Serves 10

VEAL PHILLIPE (Riviera Hotel)

The chef at the Ristorante Delmonico recommends serving the Veal Phillipe over a bed of combined spinach and white fettucine. Pounded chicken breast halves may be substituted for the veal scallopini.

6 tablespoons clarified butter (see below)
12 2-ounce slices veal scallopini
flour
1 tablespoon minced shallots
2 cups red wine
¼ cup minced green onion
½ cup peeled and chopped tomatoes
½ cup sliced mushrooms, sautéed
1½ cups brown sauce
½ cup beef broth
1 teaspoon minced garlic
½ teaspoon oregano
1 teaspoon sweet basil
2 tablespoons fresh lemon juice
1 pinch crushed red pepper
salt
white pepper
2 tablespoons unsalted butter

In a large skillet heat clarified butter until bubbly. Dust veal lightly with flour and sauté on both sides until lightly browned. Remove veal to a warm platter and pour off excess grease from skillet. Add shallots to same pan and sauté lightly. Add red wine and deglaze pan over medium-high heat. Allow wine to reduce to ½ cup. Add green onion, tomato, mushrooms and cook for 30 seconds. Add brown sauce, beef broth, garlic, oregano, basil, lemon juice, red pepper, salt and pepper. Continue to cook until sauce has been reduced to 1½ cups. Remove from heat and stir in unsalted butter. Allow three slices of veal per person. Top each serving with sauce.

Serves 4

Clarified butter is merely butter with the white milk solids removed. It is used in cooking because it has a higher burning temperature. To clarify butter, simply melt butter in a saucepan over moderate heat. Skim off the foam at the surface and pour off the yellow liquid from the "milky" residue. Discard the milky residue. Clarified butter when refrigerated keeps indefinitely, so it might be a good idea to make plenty to have on hand.

GRENADINE OF VEAL NORMANDIE *(Sands Hotel)*

This entrée is featured in the hotel's gourmet restaurant, The Regency Room. The chef recommends serving it with fresh asparagus and wild rice.

1½	pounds veal scallops
	salt
	white pepper
	flour
4	tablespoons clarified butter (see Index)
1	shallot, finely diced
1	tablespoon applejack brandy
1	cup Chablis
2	cups heavy cream
1	apple, sliced and poached in sugar and water
	parsley sprigs

Season veal with salt and pepper. Dredge lightly with flour, shaking off excess. Heat butter in a heavy skillet over medium-high heat and sauté veal 3 minutes on each side. As the veal is cooked remove from the skillet to a warm platter. Drain most of the butter from the skillet and add diced shallots. Cook approximately 1 minute. Flambé the shallots in the skillet with the brandy. Add the Chablis and continue to cook over high heat until wine is reduced by half. Lower heat, add cream, and simmer until sauce thickens and coats a spoon. Pour the sauce over the veal and garnish with sliced apples and parsley sprigs.

Serves 4

CHICKEN VESUVIUS *(Four Queens Hotel)*

Hugo's Cellar complements this dish with crisp potato skins, sour cream and freshly steamed vegetables with herb butter. If you plan to prepare this dish don't forget to begin a day ahead of time to allow for marinating.

8	chicken breast halves, skinned and boned
2	cups olive oil
2	tablespoons chopped shallots
6	tablespoons minced garlic
½	bay leaf
¼	teaspoon thyme
⅛	teaspoon oregano
½	teaspoon sweet basil
⅛	teaspoon rosemary
¼	teaspoon pepper
¼	teaspoon Tabasco

Flatten the boned chicken breasts between waxed paper with a meat cleaver or rolling pin until they are ½-inch thick. Combine all remaining ingredients. Mix well and pour into a shallow 9 × 13-inch ovenproof dish. Place chicken in this mixture and marinate overnight in the refrigerator. Turn occasionally. Bake chicken in marinade in a preheated 425° oven for 10 to 12 minutes or until done (if you wish, you may remove half of the marinade before cooking). When serving, lace some of the heated marinade over the chicken.

Serves 4

CHICKEN GRANDMÈRE *(Dunes Hotel and Country Club)*

The chef noted that an accompaniment of glazed carrots would complete this entrée. It is prepared by the hotel only upon special request.

1	3-4 pound chicken
2	tablespoons butter or margarine
3	carrots, chopped
2	onions, chopped
3	stalks celery, chopped
½	bay leaf, crumbled
¼	teaspoon rosemary
¼	teaspoon thyme
	salt
	pepper
3	slices bacon, chopped
¼	pound pearl onions, peeled
6	medium potatoes, peeled and cut into balls with a melon baller
	vegetable oil
½	cup flour
½	cup Sherry
2	cups chicken broth

Rub the chicken with butter. Place it in a roasting pan and surround with carrots, onions and celery. Season with bay leaf, rosemary, thyme, salt and pepper. Roast on the middle rack of a preheated 375° oven for 1 hour or until done. While chicken is roasting, sauté bacon with pearl onions and potatoes in a large skillet for approximately 20 minutes or until onions and potatoes are tender. Stir frequently. Add oil sparingly to pan if vegetables begin to stick. Cover and set aside. When chicken is done, remove to a platter and keep warm. Surround chicken with pearl onions and potatoes. To the pan drippings add ½ cup flour. Over medium heat cook 3 to 4 minutes stirring constantly. Add Sherry and chicken broth and return to a boil. Cook until the mixture is slightly thickened and the gravy is smooth. Strain gravy, add to cooked chicken.

Serves 4

Just for fun, design a centerpiece with fresh clippings from your own backyard. Let the season dictate what you will choose: ivy, autumn leaves, pine boughs, or pyracantha—the list goes on.

CHICKEN BREAST PORTOFINO
(Desert Inn Country Club and Spa)

A specialty of the Portofino, this entrée goes well with Stracciatella alla Romana (consommé), a hearts of palm salad, and a light pasta.

1	cup buttermilk
	salt
	pepper
4	chicken breast halves, skinned and boned
	flour
5	tablespoons olive oil
¼	pound fresh mushrooms, sliced
1	garlic clove, minced
2	tablespoons pine nuts
¼	cup dry white wine
¼	cup chicken broth
	parsley

Season buttermilk with salt and pepper. Place chicken breasts in seasoned milk and refrigerate for 2 hours turning occasionally. When ready to cook, drain chicken and dust with flour. In a skillet over medium heat sauté the breasts in 4 tablespoons of the olive oil for 5 minutes per side. Remove from heat. In another skillet over medium heat sauté mushrooms and garlic in the remaining 1 tablespoon of olive oil. Add pine nuts, wine and chicken broth to the sauce. Stir well and continue to cook until sauce has been reduced slightly. Add sautéed chicken, cover, and simmer over low heat 5 to 8 minutes or until chicken is done. Sprinkle with fresh parsley and serve.

Serves 2 to 4

FIRESIDE FRIENDSHIP AFTER-THE-SHOW

Pomegranate Cordials

Chocolate Lover's Heaven

French Lace Cookies

Crescent Cookies

Frosted Banana Spice Cookies

Demitasse

Delicious, make-ahead desserts are the star attractions for this after-the-show gathering around the warming fireplace.

Tableware provided by Broadway Southwest Department Store

BREAST OF CHICKEN SICILIANO (Barbary Coast Hotel)

Michael's Gourmet Restaurant presents this Italian chicken with fresh steamed broccoli and vermicelli cooked al dente.

8	chicken breast halves, skinned and boned
	salt
	pepper
	flour
	olive oil
4	tablespoons butter
2	tablespoons minced shallots
1	teaspoon minced garlic
2	cups thinly sliced fresh mushrooms
2	6-ounce jars marinated artichoke hearts, drained
24	whole black olives
¾	cup dry white wine
	juice of one lemon
4	thin slices prosciutto, julienned
	minced parsley

Season chicken with salt and pepper. Dust chicken in flour. In a heavy skillet heat ¼-inch oil. Sauté chicken until golden brown on both sides. Reduce heat and cook slowly until done. Remove chicken from skillet and keep warm. Drain oil from skillet. Combine butter, shallots, garlic, mushrooms, artichoke hearts, olives and wine in the skillet. Add lemon juice to taste. Simmer slowly until heated through. Return chicken to skillet and reheat. Transfer chicken to a warmed platter. Spoon sauce over chicken and garnish with prosciutto and parsley. Enjoy!

Serves 4

To reflect your culinary talents and the candles' glow, use 12-inch mirrored tiles as place mats for that gala dinner. (They are available at hardware and home improvement centers.) To protect your table from scratching, glue felt on the tile bottoms.

SPAGHETTI ALLA CARBONARA *(Las Vegas Hilton Hotel)*

This recipe is a house specialty at the hotel's Italian restaurant Leonardo's. Like any traditional pasta dish it is wonderful with just salad and bread. For a more elaborate fare it makes a wonderful accompaniment to a shrimp entrée.

¾ pound spaghetti
½ cup chicken broth
1 ounce dry white wine
1 garlic clove, minced
½ cup butter
4 slices bacon, cooked and crumbled
   salt
   ground black pepper
¾ cup freshly grated Parmesan cheese
2 egg yolks, beaten

Cook spaghetti al dente. Drain and keep warm. (Do not rinse spaghetti.) In a large skillet combine chicken broth, wine, garlic, butter and bacon. Bring mixture to a boil. Season with salt and pepper. Add the warm spaghetti and toss well. Finally add Parmesan cheese and egg yolks. Toss again and serve on warm plates.

Serves 2 to 4

SCAMPI FINES HERBES *(Tropicana Hotel)*

This quick to prepare main dish is featured in the Rhapsody Room. Serve the scampi with rice pilaf or linguini.

1 tablespoon finely chopped shallots
½ tablespoon minced garlic
½ cup clarified butter (see Index)
12 large raw shrimp, peeled and deveined
2 tablespoons brandy
¼ teaspoon oregano
¼ teaspoon basil
½ teaspoon minced fresh parsley
¼ cup dry white wine
¾ cup canned tomatoes, drained and diced
   salt
   pepper

In a large skillet over medium heat sauté shallots and garlic in clarified butter until transparent but not brown. Add shrimp and cook until shrimp turns pink. Slowly pour brandy into skillet and cook 30 seconds. (If your skillet is very hot, the brandy may ignite. Therefore, add it very carefully to avoid being burned.) Add all remaining ingredients and simmer for 5 minutes. Season to taste.

Serves 2

FIESTA TAMALE PIE *(Landmark Hotel)*

The Landmark Hotel serves this entrée for catered Mexican buffets. It doubles easily if you are serving a "real" crowd.

2	lbs. ground beef
½	lb. ground pork
2	medium onions, chopped
2	garlic cloves, minced
2	16-ounce cans whole tomatoes (use crushed or diced if you prefer)
2	16-ounce cans whole kernel corn, drained
45	whole pitted ripe olives
2½	teaspoons salt
6	teaspoons chili powder
4	eggs, beaten
2	cups milk
2	cups yellow cornmeal
2	cups shredded American cheese

In a 4 or 5-quart Dutch oven, sauté meat, onion and garlic until tender. Stir in tomatoes, corn, olives, salt and chili powder. Bring mixture to a boil and then pour into a very large casserole (or 2 smaller casseroles). In a separate bowl combine eggs, milk and cornmeal. Mix well and spoon over meat mixture. Sprinkle cheese on top. Bake in a preheated 350° oven for 45 minutes.

Serves 16

Here is an idea for an unusual, but practical hostess gift. Using nylon thread, string together red and yellow chile peppers and allow to dry. Add a bow—OLÉ!

PEAR CHARLOTTE MANFRED *(Caesars Palace Hotel)*

This is a glorious dessert for a large party, and that is exactly what Caesars Palace reserves it for: special gatherings and private parties. We used Williams Pear Brandy in the recipe; unique because it contains a whole full-grown pear. However, you may use any other brand of pear brandy and "skip" the step of "breaking the bottle". Do not add an additional pear to the poaching liquid.

TO POACH PEARS

1½ cups sugar
1   quart water
    rind of 1 lemon
1   vanilla bean
1   cinnamon stick
    pear from Williams Pear Brandy bottle
9   Bosc pears, peeled

Combine sugar, water, lemon rind, vanilla bean and cinnamon stick. Drain brandy from the bottle and reserve. Add pear from the bottle to poaching liquid. (Yes, you will have to break the bottle.) Bring liquid to a simmer and add pears. Return to a simmer and poach for 8 to 12 minutes or until fork-tender (timing depends upon the firmness and ripeness of the pears). Remove the 9 Bosc pears, pat dry and cool. Dice 3 of the pears and quarter 6 of them lengthwise. Set aside.

CHARLOTTE FILLING

22 egg yolks
1¾ cups sugar
8   tablespoons gelatin
3   cups Williams Pear Brandy
8   cups heavy cream, whipped
    butter

In a mixing bowl beat the egg yolks and add sugar slowly until the mixture is stiff. Transfer to the top of a double boiler and heat slowly to 212° on a candy thermometer, stirring constantly. (This step may take up to an hour. Be patient and cautious at this point or you will have 22 scrambled egg yolks.) In a saucepan combine the gelatin and brandy and heat to dissolve. Let cool slightly. Add the brandy mixture to the sugar and egg yolks. Whip until cool. Fold whipped cream into the egg mixture, then fold in the diced pears. Butter 3 charlotte molds and place in the freezer 1 to 2 minutes for butter to set. Remove and fill with pear mixture. Refrigerate until set.

(continued on next page)

CHOCOLATE GLAZE

10 ounces semi-sweet chocolate
3   tablespoons vegetable
    shortening

Melt chocolate and shortening in the top of a double boiler. Let cool slightly. Arrange quartered pears on a baking sheet that has been covered with waxed paper. Using a large spoon drizzle glaze over pears covering completely. Let set for 45 minutes.

RASPBERRY SAUCE

4   cups raspberries (thawed if
    frozen)
2½ cups sugar
¼   cup eau-de-vie Framboise,
    Kirsch, or raspberry juice

Combine the raspberries, sugar and liqueur in a blender. Blend well and refrigerate.

ASSEMBLY

    whipped cream
    chocolate ornaments
    (optional)

Unmold the charlottes onto serving platters. Arrange 8 pear quarters on top of each charlotte, narrow ends pointing to the center. Using a pastry bag, decorate with stiffly beaten whipped cream. The chef also suggests decorating the charlottes with chocolate ornaments. Refrigerate. Top with raspberry sauce when serving.

Serves 30 to 40

BANANA FRITTERS (*Flamingo Hilton Hotel*)

This dessert is served in the hotel's Peking Market. Our taste testers enthusiastically agreed with the chef, with "gobs" of whipped cream, it is irresistible!

4   tablespoons flour
1   teaspoon peanut oil
1   egg
8   tablespoons water
    pinch of baking powder
2   large bananas, peeled and
    quartered
4   tablespoons cornstarch
    oil for deep frying
1¼ cups heavy cream, whipped

Combine flour, oil, egg, water and baking powder in a bowl. Mix well. Roll banana quarters in cornstarch, then dip in batter. Deep fry bananas until evenly golden brown and serve with freshly whipped cream.

Serves 4 to 6

BRANDIED PEACH HALVES (*MGM Grand Hotel*)

If ordered in advance, the gourmet room Gigi's will serve this recipe as an appetizer. The chef also commented that it is equally as good grilled and used as a garnish. This recipe holds nicely for several days.

4-5 29-ounce cans peach halves
    in heavy syrup
    (approximately 12 cups)
50 whole cloves
12 ounces liquid brown sugar
1   cup pineapple juice
6   cinnamon sticks
1   10-ounce jar maraschino
    cherries (approximately 35),
    partially drained
1   cup diced crystallized ginger
1   cup brandy or rum

In a 6-quart pot combine all ingredients and mix well. Cover and refrigerate overnight, stirring occasionally. For presentation place a cherry inside each peach half.

Serves 30 to 35

GRAPEFRUIT SURPRISE À LA SAHARA *(Sahara Hotel)*

4   small whole grapefruits
12   ounces fresh blackberries (frozen and thawed, or canned and drained blackberries may be substituted)
½   cup powdered sugar
3   tablespoons blackberry liqueur or brandy
5   tablespoons sugar
1   egg white
2   tablespoons chopped hazelnuts, skins removed (see Index)

Cut a slice from the top of each grapefruit and scoop out the flesh. Remove and discard the cores and any pith and seeds from the flesh. Chop the flesh and combine with the blackberries. Stir in powdered sugar and liqueur. Fill the grapefruit shells with this mixture and chill for 20 minutes. Beat the egg white with 2½ tablespoons of the sugar until stiff. Top the stuffed grapefruit with this mixture. Broil until meringue is lightly golden. In a small saucepan melt the remaining 2½ tablespoons of sugar. Add the hazelnuts and stir well. Sprinkle over the meringue and serve.

Serves 4

Index

Contributors

The Junior League of Las Vegas wishes to gratefully acknowledge the many members, relatives and friends who submitted recipes and gave so generously of their time and talents to make *Winning at the Table* possible.

Gloria Abrums	Barbara Burns	Kay Dorn	Terry Harrison
Jeanne Ackerman	Pearl Busch	Julie Doyle	Debby Hartley
Anna Adams	Florence Lee Cahlan	Ruth Dreitz	Judy Hartman
Trudy Adams	Kristine Cahlan	Pat Dulin	Nancy Heberlee
Delia Addine	Pam Callahan	Trudy Duncan	Barbara Henry
Mary Addine	Daphne Campbell	Leslie Dunsworth	June Herrling
Barbara Alderfer	Sharon Carelli	Helen Early	Mary Lou Herrling
Janice Haupt Allen	Paul Carelli III	Martha Edwards	Mary Hirsch
Margaret Allen	Mary Carpi	Ilse Epprecht	Edna Hoffman
Mary Almquist	Martha Carter	Mary Eshragh	Karen Hohl
Donna Andress	Sharon Carter	Nancy Etter	Jane Hollingsworth
Madeleine Andress	Linda Casey	Toni Fain	Betsy Horne
Lillian Argyle	Rebecca Casey	Marla Fair	Lynn Houseal
Cathy Askew	Mary Cashman	Christy Falba	Jeanne Howerton
Melinda Auten	Alison Cawley	Linda Fahringer	Dorothy Huffey
Lisa Babcock	Gae Chalker	Kelly Fleming	Paul Huffey
Pat Baldwin	Carolyn Celeste	Helene Follmer	Karlene Hundrop
Sharon Beatty	Rikki Cheese	Deborah Ford	Marti Impagliazzo
Donna Becker	Marcia Chin	Elaine Frazier	Barbara Ingersoll
Chris Beecroft	Sue Fawn Chung	Lynn Freeman	Christy Jones
Ardie Beeler	Judy Ciliax	Nancy Galyean	Nancy Joslin
Beverly Beich	Jeanette Clark	Peggie Gambarana	Phyllis Joslin
Barbara Beier	Laura Clontz	Nancy Gasho	D. J. Kartes
Patricia Beitz	Sherry Colquitt	Gail Gilpin	Diane Keating
Linda Bixler	Janet Coombs	Luanne Glenn	Marlys Kellogg
Judy Blaisdell	Beda Cornwall	Barbara Gnatovich	Marianne Kifer
Mary Blake	Estelle Corrigan	Lucille Goodman	Marlyne Kirshbaum
Eunice Boles	Nancy Corrigan	Marilyn Glovinsky	Laurie Koelliker
Jeane Boman	Cathy Cox	Joanne Goldberg	Joanmarie Kolesar
Jean Borders	Bernadine Creer	Susan Graves	Adele Koot
Eileen Borellis	Caty Crockett	Darlene Green	Monica Laman
Jane Boudreau	Pattie Crockett	Jan Greene	Peg Lamkin
Diane Brady	Jean Curran	Theresa Griffin	Chelette Laporta
Diane Brandise	Sonja Curtis	Dinah Groce	Eleissa Lavelle
Monty Brandt	Cindy Daileda	Kitty Groce	Bonnie Lawyer
Mannetta Braunstein	Kathy Dalvey	Rita Gubler	Richard Layne
Madge Brockman	Beverly Daly	Corky Guercio	Sherry Layne
Jeanne Brooker	Sarah Danzinger	Marti Hafen	Doris Lebo
Sue Brooks	Mary Davies	Clark Hafen	Nancy Leslie
Frances Brown	Deborah Debeauchamp	Sandra Halseth	Gloria Lewton
Pam Brown	Jackie Delanoy	Vicki Ham	Jimmye Livingston
Shirley Brown	Sara Denton	Jan Hanes	Marilyn Loop
Judy Brusa	Karen Diamond	Peggy Hanley	Patricia Luetkehans
Lynn Buchanan	Doree Dickerson	Mary Hanigan	Andra Maffey
Cathy Buckley	Peggy Dickerson	Sheila Harding	Charold Mahan
Lee Burnett	Ann Dilley	Mary Alice Hardy	Kathleen Mahon

Gerda Malamud
Joy Mandekic
Marolyn Mann
Lana Manos
Sandra Marnell
Lois McClanathan
Nancy McGroarty
Trudy McLaren
Ann McNamee
Susan Menelaides
Nancy Millard
Debbie Miller
Mary Jo Miller
Doreen Mills
Julie Milne
Madelyn Montgomery
Pat Morrison
Darlene Muterspaw
Dedee Nave
Nancy Neville
Linda Nitzschke
Dal Nua
Candace Olson
Rene O'Reilly
Sherlene Parson
Verona Pasquale
Gloria Pearson
Cindy Pechman
Nancy Peccole
Patricia Peltz
Mary Perkowski
Mary Pinjuv

Helene Powell
Eva Pruter
Lali Publow
Maria Quirk
Donalene Ravitch
Karlene Reed
Nina Reitz
Milly Remy
Betsy Rhodes
Genevieve Rice
Karen Rice
Saundra Richardson
Mary Ann Rivera
Cheryl Rogers
Rita Rohbauch
Dede Rosenthal
Kellie Rubin
Carol Rumbolz
Elizabeth Ruybalid
Glenna Ryan
Erin Scalley
Megan Scalley
Priscilla Scalley
Mary Scheer
Blair Scoville
Sandra Seiler
Kim Sennes
Jo Ann Shiroff
Charlene Scott
Nancy Shepherd
Betty Sherlock
Tona Siefert

Hilda Silman
Linda Silvestri
Barbara Simes
Jule Simon
Sydnee Smith
Arlene Southard
Carolyn Sparks
Sharon Spaulding
Jan Sprague
Patty Steirhoff
Cindy Stewart
Patricia Stow
John Stuart
Suzie Stuart
Deborah Swissman
Judy Sylvain
Marlene Sylvain
Zetta Sylvain
Beth Sylvester
Jan Tait
Pam Taylor
Carla Thompson
Joyce Thompson
Kathryn Thompson
Kathy Thompson
Dixie Thorne
Sandra Tiberti
Nancy Tiffany
Barbara Tipe
Janice Titus
Joan Tracht
Ken Tracht

Judy Trent
Suzanne van Aken
Chloe van Buren
Jackie Vaughan
Charleen Vega
Rose Villada
Doris Wade
Linda Wade
Linda Wadell
Colleen Wadhams
Pamela Wald
Jeri Wallis
Jane Walter
Gail Warthen
Janice Warthen
Norma Warthen
Marion Washington
Lynn Wiesner
Carolyn Wilson
Diana Wilson
Bill Winchester
Gretchen Winchester
Lynn Wirth
Gen Wirth
Roger Wirth
Lynda Wohletz
Sharon Wolfram
Dolly Woo
Bonnie Woodcock
Christine Worrell
Lou Ann Young
Betty Zahn

We also extend a special thank you to the many hotels who contributed recipes.

Barbary Coast Hotel
Caesars Palace Hotel
Desert Inn Country Club and Spa
Dunes Hotel and Country Club
Flamingo Hilton Hotel
Four Queens Hotel
Frontier Hotel

Landmark Hotel
Las Vegas Hilton Hotel
MGM Grand Hotel
Riviera Hotel
Sahara Hotel
Sands Hotel
Tropicana Hotel

Winning at the Table

Junior League of Las Vegas Publications
P. O. Box 43419
Las Vegas, Nevada 89116

Please send _____ copies of *Winning at the Table*   @ *$14.95* each $ _____
Postage and handling   @   *2.00* each $ _____
Gift wrap and enclosure card from _____   @   *1.00* each $ _____
                                                          TOTAL $ _____

Please make checks payable to the *Junior League of Las Vegas Publications*.

NAME _____

ADDRESS _____

CITY _____ STATE _____ ZIP _____

- -

Winning at the Table

Junior League of Las Vegas Publications
P. O. Box 43419
Las Vegas, Nevada 89116

Please send _____ copies of *Winning at the Table*   @ *$14.95* each $ _____
Postage and handling   @   *2.00* each $ _____
Gift wrap and enclosure card from _____   @   *1.00* each $ _____
                                                          TOTAL $ _____

Please make checks payable to the *Junior League of Las Vegas Publications*.

NAME _____

ADDRESS _____

CITY _____ STATE _____ ZIP _____

- -

Winning at the Table

Junior League of Las Vegas Publications
P. O. Box 43419
Las Vegas, Nevada 89116

Please send _____ copies of *Winning at the Table*   @ *$14.95* each $ _____
Postage and handling   @   *2.00* each $ _____
Gift wrap and enclosure card from _____   @   *1.00* each $ _____
                                                          TOTAL $ _____

Please make checks payable to the *Junior League of Las Vegas Publications*.

NAME _____

ADDRESS _____

CITY _____ STATE _____ ZIP _____